MORALS, LAW
AND LIFE

CAHAL B. DALY

Father Daly was born at Loughguile, Co. Antrim and studied at St. Malachy's College, Belfast, at Queen's University, at Maynooth and in Paris. He graduated B.A. in 1936 and M.A. in 1937 (in Ancient Classics) at Queen's University. He was ordained at Maynooth in 1941. He obtained his D.D. at Maynooth in 1944 for a study on *Turtullian the Puritan and his Influence,* extracts from which were published in the *Irish Ecclesiastical Record* between 1947 and 1950. He obtained his L.Ph. at the Institut Catholique, Paris, in 1953. He has been Lecturer in Scholastic Philosophy in Queen's University since 1946 and was appointed Reader in 1962.

He was a *Peritus* of the Second Vatican Council. Besides *Morals, Law and Life,* Fr. Daly has contributed a chapter to *Prospect for Metaphysics* (London 1961); and articles on theological (chiefly patristic), on philosophical and on moral subjects, with special reference to existentialist philosophy and to contemporary British linguistic philosophy and moral philosophy, chiefly in the *Irish Theological Quarterly* and in *Philosophical Studies.* He has been Chairman of the Christus Rex, a society of Irish priests for social study and action, since its inception in 1941.

MORALS, LAW AND LIFE

BY

CAHAL B. DALY, M.A.,D.D.
Reader in Scholastic Philosophy,
Queen's University, Belfast

240
DA

SCEPTER
CHICAGO — DUBLIN — LONDON

PUBLISHER'S NOTE

A so called "New Morality" which goes hand in hand with the God-is-dead theology is now reaching the popular level. One cannot pick up a magazine today without being exposed to its appalling logic and complete distortion of the Gospel's message (whenever a particular author chooses to use the Gospel). However, there is nothing new and certainly no morality in this movement as *Morals, Law and Life* will show.

The book was originally published in Ireland by Clonmore and Reynolds from a series of articles which had appeared in the *Irish Theological Quarterly,* in which Dr. Daly answered *The Sancity of Life and the Criminal Law,* by Dr. Glanville Williams. Dr. Williams, a Cambridge (England) lawyer received much acclaim throughout the English-speaking world and his book has come to be accepted as a typical statement and a powerful vindication of the liberal-agnostic or scientific-humanist ethic.

Dr. Daly's work is primarily an examination of Dr. Williams's book. It takes account also of other influential expositions of the "new morality" philosophy of life, especially of Bertrand Russsell's still best-selling *Marriage and Morals* and of a curiously similar book, *Morals and Medicine* by Rev.

3

Joseph Fletcher, professor at the Episcopal Theological School in Cambridge, Mass.

The purpose of the present book is not, however, merely critical. It has a positive aim, to show
forth the truth and beauty and nobility of the
Church's view of sex, of love, of marriage and
parenthood, of life, suffering and death.

Dr. Daly, one might ask, ought to have revised
the book in light of more recent problematic, discussion and writing on the subject of birth regulation? He believes, however, that the argument of
this book is just as valid now, though he would
wish to adopt a more irenic style. An attempt to
deal with some aspects of the more recent literature
will be found in his *Natural Law Morality Today,*
published in the December 1965 issue of *The
American Ecceliastical Review.*

However, this book *Morals, Law and Life* can
have more force in the light of the "progress" made
by the anti-life groups. Today the abundance of
articles soft-selling abortion grows by leaps and
bounds. The purely subjective and very narrow
view of this problem is the one taken by most of
these writings. The seed sown, or rather watered
by Dr. Williams's book is now bearing abundant
fruit.

There must be "equal time" of positive literature
on morality, on law and above all on life. The pub-
lisher hopes that Dr. Daly's book might be one
grain of seed on the American scene which, when
read by reasonable men, may be carrried to fertile

ground and yield good fruit, which in turn will throw a sane light on the confusion of ideas swimming helter skelter under the label of "new morality" in our society today.

Chicago, March 7, 1966

AUTHOR'S FOREWORD

Dr. Glanville Williams is Lecturer in Law and Fellow of Jesus College, Cambridge. A Welshman, born in 1911, he was educated at St. John's College, Cambridge, and was a Research Fellow there from 1936 until 1942. He received his L.L.D. in 1946. He became successively Reader in English Law, Professor of Public Law and Quain Professor of Jurisprudence in the University of London, 1945-1955. He returned to Cambridge in 1955. He was Carpentier Lecturer in the Columbia Law School and at the Association of the Bar of the City of New York in Spring, 1956; and it is from this lectureship that the book, *The Sanctity of Life and the Criminal Law,* is derived. It was published in America in 1956. The British edition (published by Faber and Faber), with some revisions, appeared in 1958. Dr. Glanville Williams is the author of many articles and studies on law, his best-known work hitherto being *Criminal Law: The General Part* (1953). He enjoys a considerable reputation and influence in certain legal circles because of his views on law reform. His latest book, therefore, attracted much attention and received great publicity on both sides of the Atlantic.

It was with considerable interest that one opened this book, expecting to find in it a fresh and scholarly examination of the relations between law and morals touching human life. One is, however, sadly disappointed in these expectations. The book

7

is lacking in both knowledge and understanding in matters of theology; it has serious inaccuracies in the statement of Catholic doctrine and in matters of historical fact. One feels driven to place it definitely outside the category of scholarly writing. Its propagandist tactics, its pervasive bias against Catholic teaching, seem to decide its place in literature.

But then, with surprise, one noted that the book was being taken very seriously indeed in some quarters. It was not only the publishers' blurb which spoke of it as a "profoundly serious" book, shedding "an intense new light" on vital moral issues "by tapping the resources of biology and medicine as well as the law, by re-examining the traditional attitude of religion and ethics . . ."; giving us "for the first time in book form, a full and balanced account, by a distinguished authority, of all aspects of the subject." Publishers' blurbs are easily forgiven. But serious reviewers command more attention; and many of these have joined in a chorus of praise, of which the following quotation from the *Times Literary Supplement* is a sample:

> Some of his readers may disagree with him strongly over certain of his interpretations of historic development, over his analysis of the present attitude of public opinion, or over his suggested reforms. But it is impossible not to be grateful for this serious and gallant effort to produce an atmosphere of greater tolerance and humanitarian compassion . . .

This may be taken as typifying the view that Dr. Glanville Williams's book represents an original contribution to legal and moral thinking; that it poses a serious problem for, throws down an important new challenge to, Catholic moralists; that a fair and intelligent debate is opened in which no one can doubt at least the deep moral seriousness, the scholarly responsibility, the conscientiousness of Dr. Glanville Williams.

We shall maintain that, in every particular, these claims made for Dr. Glanville Williams are unjustifiable; we hope to prove that our first impressions, described above, are in fact a true and just assessment of the book. Before examing in detail his treatment of different medico-moral problems, we think it well first to introduce Dr. Glanville Williams to readers by quoting some specimen passages and summarizing some of his typical pieces of theological discussion. These will be a fair introductory sample enabling readers to judge of the author's supposed detachment, scholarship and sense of responsibility, as well as to savour his brand of humanism. To some of these passages we shall have to return later, when examination of the moral argument requires it.

We hesitate to reproduce some of these passages, which must deeply shock and wound decent people. It is, however, necessary to do so, in order to show just what the protagonists of Dr. Glanville Williams are defending and just what is the nature of the "imaginative humanitarianism" which the author wishes to substitute for the Church's "authoritarian dogmatism" and "doctrinaire conservatism."

CONTENTS

1

Lawyer, Moralist or Theologian?

The first passage which we quote to illustrate the tone of the book is one which no Catholic reader will be able soon to forget. The author writes:

A biblical argument in favour of artificial insemination could easily be constructed by showing that it is the only form of virtuous propagation on the woman's side, being entirely free from sinful lust and approximating to the immaculate conception.[1]

We feel that if Dr. Glanville Williams had known what the words meant, he would never have written this unworthy sentence. It is, however, obvious enough that he simply did not know what he was saying; his ignorance of Christian teaching is clamant. But there is ignorance which is inexcusable. It would have been so simple to find out what the words "immaculate conception" mean. It would have been so easy for the writer to avoid giving insult to the faith of millions of his country-men, to speak only of them. There are aspects of his subject about

13

which Dr. Glanville Williams has professional competence. He should have confined himself to these.

But throughout his whole book he persists in embarking on theological discussions and arguments for which he has not the most elementary equipment. His treatment of the doctrine of original sin is typical of his qualifications as a theologian. In a book which he has read on the subject,[2] he has learned that the doctrine "appears to have been the invention of Origen," who could think up no other explanation of the nascent custom of infant Baptism! The theory was taken up by St. Augustine and rapidly "became orthodox Christian doctrine."[3] Scientifically, "the doctrine of original sin might (now) seem to be deprived of its last vestige of rational support"; because "the great majority of biologists are firm against the inheritance of acquired characteristics."[4] A great deal of Catholic medical ethics originated in this pre-scientific dogma and was aroused by the horror of unborn infants suffering "eternal punishment" if they died without the "magical" rite of baptism.[5] There are signs, however, of a gradual decline of superstition even among Catholics, at least of the educated sort.

> The Catholic rules of emergency baptism may perhaps be regarded at the present day as concessions to the faith of the more unsophisticated members of the sect, for the Roman priesthood seems to have surrendered the distinctively religious or eschatological approach to the problem of abortion and to

base itself instead upon the less vulnerable doctrine of natural rights.[6]

Therefore, as science spreads among them, the accession of Catholics to a civilized outlook on many matters is by no means to be despaired of. In fact, the Pope has, recently, quietly got away with "a partial renunciation of the mischevious dogma of original sin," when he "announced that there was nothing sinful in new technics of painless childbirth."[7]

It is, for his own sake and that of his friends, a pity that Dr. Glanville Williams did not show these passages to some Catholic before letting them be printed. Almost any "unsophisticated member of the sect" could have kept him from making himself so ridiculous in public. It is ironic that blunders of this order about the beliefs of the Trobriand Islanders would have exposed their author to the derision of the learned world; the beliefs of primitive peoples are Science . . .! It is deplorable that, in otherwise educated Anglo-Saxon circles to-day, one can get away undetected with such errors about the tenets of the Faith which made Europe and created its greatest art, philosophy and literature and inspires to-day a majority of its most intelligent and civilized minds.

But Dr. Glanville Williams does not wish to understand or to be just to Catholic teaching; he only wishes to destroy it. His technique is a perfect example of the use of "persuasive definitions"[7a]; he does not argue or reason, he simply affixes a "smear-word" to Catholic doctrines, which he does not like, and a "cheer-word" to the opposed practices, which he does like. It is the technique, so familiar to us, of the propagandist. This is not argument; it is advertising.

Examples of the technique occur on every alternate page. To give references would be tedious. Christian moral teaching is "reactionary," "old-fashioned," "unimaginative," "primitive if not blasphemous," "restrictive," "irrational," "outmoded," "dogmatic, doctrinaire," "authoritarian." Contrasted with it are "enlightened opinion," "interesting medico-social experimentation," "progressive statutes," "empirical, imaginative humanitarianism." Christianity is "morbid, guilt-ridden," "anti-sexual," has a "sadistic God," is pervaded with "masochism," desires "to thwart natural impulses merely for the sake of thwarting them";[8] advances "the sour doctrines that all indulgence of the sexual impulses is libidinous sin";[9] preaches resignation, i.e. "that the more unpleasant of two alternatives has some intrinsic moral superiority," stands opposed to the belief "that laughter is better than sorrow."[10] "Religious masochism . . . fatalism" are words that come constantly to his lips. As authority for these charges, he seems to rely on Lecky and Westermarck. He has, indeed, a curious predilection for books of history and anthropology dating from the first decade of the century.

As a propagandist he is, however, quite contemporary. He speaks once of "religious terrorism," and here we seem to hear a familiar voice; and we realize how limited, after all, is the vocabulary of the propagandists and how poor their common stock of ideas. But Dr. Glanville Williams has undeniable expertise. It is a real *tour de force* to label Catholic teaching "theocratic," since it believes in God as Author of the moral law; and "sectarian," since it is rejected by some non-Catholics. These are show-pieces of emotive question-begging; of what R. L. Thouless called "crooked thinking."

Dr. Glanville Williams has led us to expect that the alternative to the morbid doctrines of guilt-ridden, Masochistic celibates must be something grand and noble and inspiring, exalting the dignity of man; a doctrine of freedom, happiness and progress. We will proceed to examine this alternative in detail presently. Here we merely illustrate it by some citations. Any commentary of ours would merely detract from their stunning effect:

> I am not clear in my own mind that this general opinion, whether religious and secular, on the subject of the sanctity of life justifies the punishment of a mother who, finding that she has given birth to a viable monster or an idiot child, kills it . . . An eugenic killing by a mother, exactly paralleled by the bitch that kills her mis-shapen puppies, cannot confidently be pronounced immoral.[11]
>
> The propagation of poor stock is regarded by public opinion as neither a sin nor a

crime against humanity . . . There is a striking contrast between human fecklessness in
our own reproduction that the careful scientific improvement of other forms of life under man's control. No rose-grower, pigeon-
fancier or cattle-breeder would behave as
men do in their own breeding habits. "Im-
agine," says Bertrand Russell, "the feelings
of a farmer who was told that he must give
all his bull calves an equal opportunity."[12]

The donation of semen presents no problem
. . . There is nothing intrinsically wrong in
selling a part of the body, e.g. hair . . . It
seems, then, that the somewhat repellent
prospect of "human stud farms," although
one of the things to be considered in passing
(*scil*. judgment)[13] upon the aesthetics or the
social desirability of artificial insemination,
is not a conclusive argument for repressing
this practice by law. If the "human′ stud
farm" produces a sufficient overplus of
good, it can, at least on a utilitarian philosophy, be justified.[14]

A compassionate acquittal took place in
1927 when a man drowned his incurably ill
child, suffering from tuberculosis and gan-
grene of the face. He had nursed her with
devoted care, but one morning, after sitting
up with her all night, could no longer bear
to see her suffering. The jury returned a
verdict of "not guilty" of murder. In the

course of his summing up, Mr. Justice Branson said: "It is a matter which gives food for thought when one comes to consider that, had this poor child been an animal instead of a human being, so far from there being anything blameworthy in the man's action in putting an end to its suffering, he would actually have been liable to punishment if he had not done so."[15]

These are only some examples of Dr. Glanville Williams's "serious and gallant effort to produce an atmosphere of greater tolerance and humanitarian compassion." They have been chosen out of many similar passages because of a common trait, which is surely significant: on the face of them, these passages assume that what is right treatment for animals is, *eo ipso,* right treatment for men. In this and other respects Dr. Glanville Williams has performed an immense service for students of Catholic medical ethics. We have believed and said that abandonment of Catholic moral standards in the sphere of sex and conception would mean the animalization of sex, the degradation of man to the level of the sub-human. We have believed and said that abortion is murder and that principles which are invoked to justify it will equally condone infanticide, geronticide and, in fact, leave no logical reason for condemning any form of murder.

Dr. Glanville Williams has obliged us by working out to just these conclusions the logic of the anti-Catholic philosophy of sex and of life. We would never have dared to attribute to this philosophy the crude formulae which this book defends. We should have been accused of misrepresentation, we should not have been believed, if we did. Perhaps after Dr. Glanville Williams we shall be believed.

It would, however, be unjust not to acknowledge Dr. Glanville Williams's precursors, on whom he has freely drawn for ideas, arguments and garbled versions of Christian teaching. Chief among these are Bertrand Russell, whose *Marriage and Morals* was first published in 1929;[16] and the Reverend Mr. Fletcher, whose book, *Morals and Medicine,*[17] draws heavily upon Russell and whose statements of and about Christian teaching are indeed remarkable, coming as they do from the "Professor of pastoral theology and Christian ethics at the Episcopal Theological College, Cambridge, Mass." There is little about religion or morals in Glanville Williams that was not already in Fletcher; and little in Fletcher that was not anticipated by Bertrand Russell. It should, however, in fairness be said that Russell's book, shocking though it be, is a good deal more humanitarian than Dr. Glanville Williams's and rather more Christian than the Reverend Mr. Fletcher's.[18] The three authors share a common outlook and together typify the moral philosophy of scientific humanism, which puts itself forward as the main antagonist of and only alternative to Christianity in the modern world. In order to broaden the discussion to the dimensions of the school, we shall refer to the views of Russell and Fletcher, where they are relevant to the discussion of those of Dr. Glanville Williams.

It may be felt that it is unfair to concentrate, as we shall in this book concentrate, on Dr. Glanville Williams's ethical and theological arguments: this is, after all, it may be said, the book of a lawyer whose main concern is with legal reform. Now the author could, had he chosen, have discussed the case for legal reform on sociological, utilitarian or other grounds which fall within the purview of legal science. As the *Times Literary Supplement* reviewer wrote:

> To restrict or even to remove the threat of punishment from some of the matters discussed in this book would not of course be to pronounce, one way or the other, upon their moral and theological implications, highly controversial as many of them are.[19]

Dr. Glanville Williams, however, has not chosen to take this line. By far the greater part of his book is taken up precisely with the moral and theological aspects of his subject. It is only intermittently that he remembers his proper competence and speaks as a lawyer. When he does, he can speak sense. He writes: "Human law does not necessarily have to enforce the whole of morality."[20] "It is necessary to insist on the distinction between morals and law."[21] The Catholic moralist can only say that he agrees;[22] and he could have a fruitful discussion with a lawyer starting from these premises. St. Thomas Aquinas wrote:

Human law is enacted for the community in general, and in the community the majority are not perfected in virtue. Therefore human law does not prohibit all the vices which those of special virtue avoid, but only the more serious vices, which the majority of people, with ordinary virtue, can avoid; and especially those vices which injure the common good and whose prohibition is necessary for the preservation of society.[23]

Human law aims to lead men to virtue, not all at once, but gradually. Therefore it does not require of the average imperfect man the standard of perfection attained by the virtuous; i.e., it does not prohibit everything that is sinful. If it did, the average imperfect man, unable to observe the law's requirements, might fall into complete lawlessness . . . The laws would come to be despised and, through contempt of law, men might become more depraved than ever.[24]

We do not intend to analyze this teaching of Aquinas here. We quote these passages only to show that a profitable discussion could have taken place between an authority on criminal law and a Catholic moralist on questions touching the law of sexual behaviour, life and death.[25] Dr. Glanville Williams has chosen, however, to refuse this debate, and to launch instead a diatribe, involving moral philosophy, in which he is incompetent, and theology, of

which he is ignorant. Denied discussion, we must
at least expose misrepresentation.

[1] P. 132.
[2] N. P. Williams, *The Ideas of the Fall and of Original Sin,*
London, 1927: "this authoritative work," He calls it.
[3] Pp. 178-81.
[4] Pp. 28f.
[5] Pp. 178, 180.
[6] P. 180.
[7] Pp. 66 f.
[7a] The phrase was introduced by C. L. Stevenson: see his
article, "Persuasive Definitions," in *Mind,* 1938, pp. 331-350;
also his book, *Ethics and Language,* Yale University Press,
1945. Here he writes: "In any 'persuasive definition' the
term defined is a familiar one, whose meaning is both descriptive and strongly emotive. The purport of the definition
is to alter the descriptive meaning of the term . . .; but the
definition does *not* make any substantial change in the term's
emotive meaning. And the definition is used, consciously or
unconsciously, in an effort to secure, by this interplay between emotive and descriptive meaning, a redirection of
people's attitudes" (*op. cit.,* p. 210). The writing of 'scientific humanists' abounds in examples of Stevenson's point.
We return to this concept in Chapter 8.
[8] P. 69.
[9] P. 61.
[10] P. 278.
[11] P. 31.
[12] P. 83. Compare n. 139 to p. 66.
[13] There is obviously a word missing in the text.
[14] P. 134.
[15] P. 293.
[16] Our edition is published by Allen & Unwin and dated
1952.
[17] Published by Gollancz, London, 1955.
[18] The blurb describes Mr. Fletcher as a "priest." Blurbs
of and prefaces to books of this kind have a curiously
monotonous sameness. When we read of a book that "this is
one of the most valuable, if controversial, books that we
have published," dealing "bravely and outspokenly but cour-

teously" with grave moral problems, we know at once that the book is an attack on decent moral standards (if, indeed, it is not straight pornography, which is always sure to be "brave and full of high moral seriousness," too). Dr. Karl Menninger, in his Foreword, says exactly the kind of thing that friendly reviewers have said of Dr. Glanville Williams: "That the author is deeply religious and earnestly ethical no one can doubt. Some of his conclusions will be contrary to prevalent Roman Catholic convictions . . . (But) the earnestness, the scholarliness, the conscientiousness and the thoroughness of the author cannot but appeal to all . . . men of good will . . . A great contribution has been made here to philosophy, to religion, to morality and to medicine." Dr. Glanville Williams likes the Reverend Mr. Fletcher; finds his "Christian humanist approach . . . at the opposite pole from that of dogmatic and authoritarian religion." (p. 127).

[19] *Times Literary Supplement, 18th July, 1958.*

[20] P. 197.

[21] P. 210.

[22] In a recent letter, dealing with censorship of obscene publications, the Bishops of the United States wrote: "Between what is legally punishable and what is morally good there is a large gap. If we were content to accept as morally harmless whatever is not punishable by law, we would greatly lower our moral standards. It must be recognized that civil legislation is not, of itself, a sufficient criterion of morality." *Documentation Catholique,* LV (1958), n. 1278, c. 694. After the publication of the Wolfenden Report on Homosexual Offences and Prostitution (Cmnd. 247, September, 1957), the Archbishop of Westminster issued a statement of which the following is part: "The civil law takes cognisance primarily of public acts. Private acts *as such* are outside its scope. However, there are certain private acts which have public consequences in so far as they affect the common good. These acts may rightly be subject to civil law. It may be, however, that the civil law cannot efficiently control such acts without doing more harm to the common good than the acts themselves would do. In that case it may be necessary in the interests of the common good to tolerate without approving such acts. It has, for example, invariably been found that adultery or fornication (which, however

private, have clear public consequences) cannot effectively be controlled by civil law without provoking greater evils." (Quoted by Michael J. Buckley, in *Morality and the Homosexual,* Sands, London, 1959, p. 197.)

23 *Summa Theol.,* 1-2, 96, 2.

24 *Ibid.,* ad 2.

25 These questions have been discussed by a young Catholic barrister, Dr. Norman St. John Stevas, in a book, *Life, Death and The Law,* published recently (1961) by Eyre and Spottiswode.

2

Natural Law or Naturalistic Fallacy?

It is characteristic of the books we have named as typical of scientific humanism, that they concentrate their fire on the central citadel of Catholic morality, the doctrine of Natural Law. For the Reverend Mr. Fletcher, this doctrine is precisely anti-moral: it means the replacement of human freedom by "fatalism"; the subordination of persons to bodies; the reduction of sex to a "helpless submission to biological consequences"; a lowering of man to the level of animals; a turning back of the wheels of progress; a return to pre-moral barbarism.[26] In his angry and often incoherent attacks on the doctrine of Natural Law, the most consistent charges are that many things (such as spectacles and false teeth) are "unnatural" but not therefore evil; that progress consists precisely in controlling nature for man's use, not in subordinating man to nature; and that nature as such is impersonal, purposeless, unmoral, so that morality consists in liberating man from enslavement to nature. He thinks that "nature," for Natural Law moralists, means the physical world, and that "natural laws" are for the moralist, as for the physical scientist, "merely statistical or average results or incidence of inhuman or sub-human physical nature."[27] This being so, our critic triumphantly concludes that Catholic moralists are committing the "naturalistic fallacy" which G. E. Moore warned about long ago: they are forsaking "the imperative mood for the indicative mood" and converting "ethics from an enterprise in value-judgements into a descriptive discipline aimed at making human actions coincide with natural, i.e. given conditions."[28] Catholic moralists are, in plain fact, trying to deduce an *ought* from an *is;* and as any undergraduate could tell them, this is a very wicked, as well as a very mistaken thing to do.

Dr. Glanville Williams could not agree more. The Catholic doctrine of Natural Law fills him with indignation.

> The supposed connection between nature and morals . . . is completely mistaken. It is hardly necessary to point out that men do many things that are unnatural . . . Miscellaneous examples are washing, shaving, driving automobiles, building cathedrals and giving blood transfusions . . . Arguments of the type here considered, from the natural to the moral and from the unnatural to the immoral, are, in fact, only examples of the ancient confusion between "is" and "ought" . . . Catholic moralists sometimes try to put

their case more specifically by saying that contraception is not merely artificial but against nature, because it prevents the natural consequence of the sexual act. They personify nature and attribute an intention to nature which man frustrates by contraception. This extremely primitive if not blasphemous theology can perhaps be sufficiently answered by pointing out that nature evidently intends males to have beards, which intention they steadily frustrate by the use of the razor.[29]

Serious students of the moral law will hardly be impressed by this line of argument. Catholic moralists, it should hardly be necessary to point out, do not try to deduce morality from physical nature; do not pronounce morally right whatever nature does; do not equate "statistical averages" of "subhuman physical" events with the moral law. The "nature" of which they are speaking is *human* nature as a physico-spiritual whole; it is man's intelligent, rational personality. If this is not the norm of morality, we may well ask: what is? St. Thomas Aquinas wrote:

> Everything created, being subject to divine providence, is controlled and judged by God's eternal law . . . But rational beings come under the eternal law in an unique way, because they actively participate in providence, being responsible for providing for their own well-being and that of others

> . . . Hence the communication of the eternal law to rational creatures is called the natural law . . . The natural law is nothing but the specifically rational, moral way in which rational being conform their conduct to the eternal law.[30]

> Irrational animals too are subject to divine governance, as rational beings are. But the divine law is communicated to rational beings through their intellectual and rational powers. This is why the communication of divine law to rational beings is properly called (natural) *law:* for law is essentially rational. The uniform behaviour of animals is not due to reason; therefore it can be called "law" only metaphorically.[31]

It is obvious that St. Thomas does not commit a "naturalistic fallacy." He sedulously distinguishes what "is the case" in subhuman nature from what "ought to be the case" in human nature; and the latter alone is the source of natural law. But let us look at the "naturalistic fallacy" argument a little more closely. When G. E. Moore brought it forward first in 1903 it was a liberating force; it freed British ethics from a good number of utilitarian and evolutionistic sophisms; it cleared the ground for reconstruction. But Moore constructed nothing that could stand: his argument was merely destructive of error, not fertile in truth. Since his time, the argument has degenerated into a cliché, an obstacle to ethical thinking. It is becoming itself the great sterilizing semi-sophism in British ethics.

Is it true, or how far is it true, that one cannot derive *ought* from *is?* It is certainly true that one cannot, with Mill, conclude from "this is desired" (a psychological generalization), to "this is desirable, i.e. morally good" (a moral or value judgment). It is true that one cannot argue from "this is the direction of evolutionary advance," to "this is morally right"—though, despite Moore, the Waddingtons and Julian Huxleys are still doing this. It is true that one cannot argue from "the (statistically) normal contemporary Britain or American does *x*" to "it is morally normal and right to do *x*"; yet psychologists, sexologists, sociologists, lawyers are constantly doing this.

Some of the best examples of the naturalistic fallacy one could wish for are in fact to be found in the literature we are examining. Thus Bertrand Russell:

> Whatever the dangers or difficulties, we must be content to let the world go forward rather than back.[32]

The Reverend Mr. Fletcher:

> Have no fear (speaking of artificial insemination), it will be found that there are plenty of twentieth century wives. The testimony of physicians shows it.[33]

Dr. Glanville Williams:

> Contraception is now a common practice

and is, therefore, as "natural" as any other aspect of civilization.[34]

The fallacy of *ignoratio elenchi* committed in all such cases is obvious. As, G. E. Moore was always pointing out, these answers do not reply to the question asked: The question is—"Is so-and-so morally right?" The answer is: "It's the way the world is moving"; "It is contemporary"; "Practically everyone does it." But, with inexorable persistence, the moral conscience repeats: "but what I must know is whether the way the world is moving is *right;* whether it is morally *right* to be contemporary in this respect; whether what nearly everyone is doing is morally *good."* Morality throws us back inescapably on our own individual responsibility as moral persons. The naturalistic fallacy is a flight from morality; an attempt to escape from moral seriousness by a game of puns.[35]

But it is quite false to conclude from the naturalistic fallacy argument that one can never validly pass from *is* to *ought.* There is one and only one sphere of being where *is* and *ought* imply one another, and this is the sphere of human existence; just as, and because, there is only one being who is *moral* and that is man. Man is *moral* because he *is* morally. Man is the being who has-to-be, who ought-to-be what he is. Man "is" in a manner unique and special to the rational being which he is; he is, not in the "fatalistic" manner of "brute physiology and biology." He has to make himself a man, a person. He is not a being fixed and finished; he has to realize, to complete his being by action. He is-to-be-for-ends (for goods, for values) which he has to conform his being to; and in this consists his morality. Morality is man's knowing that he *ought* to *become* what he *is;* that he ought to become a man by conduct becoming to a man. It is a sheer mistake to say that an *is* can never lead to an *ought.* "What man is" is the premiss and norm for discovering what man ought to be and what man ought to do. The whole enquiry into Natural Law is an enquiry into what man is as a moral person.[36] Natural Law morality is rational, personalistic morality. It is what Russell, the Reverend Mr. Fletcher and Dr. Glanville Williams themselves appeal to in their morality of personal development and inter-personal relationships. But, as we shall show, their morality becomes inhuman and anti-personalist because of their defective understanding of the human person.

[26] Op. cit., pp. 85-99, where the author is arguing passionately for contraception as a high point in man's advance to "moral maturity." The attack on Natural Law pervades the whole book. He has one rather ingenious "plug-line" to use against Natural Law; he frequently calls it "Counter-Reformation." What this means in the context must remain obscure, but it will undoubtedly ring bells in the Bible Belt. It is, incidentally, curious how Dr. Glanville Williams, who does not profess any religious beliefs at all, nevertheless assumes that contraception, abortion, sterilization, artificial insemination and euthanasia, etc., are Progressive and Protestant; and that the Enemy is the Roman Church. See pp. 51 ff., 61-2, 72, 99, 134-5, 177.

[27] Op. cit., p. 86.

[28] Pp. 222 f. We have to place the rest of the paragraph in a footnote, because we cannot make sense of it: "When nature

rules, conscience is made of none effect and reduced to the amoral level of natural cause and effect, that is, *non compos mentis."* This may be printer's error, as also may be *de rerum nature* on p. 67; *Cura Sacra Poenitentiaria* on p. 69; *De Bono Conjugale* on p. 79; "potential life *(vitam in potentia)* if not of a life in actual being *(vitam in sit),"* p. 91. In the absence, however, of any correct Latin passages, we cannot prove this.

[29] Pp. 64-6; cf. pp. 133, 237, 238.

[30] *S. Theol.,* 1-2, 91, 2. The last sentence is a paraphrase, necessary, we think, to bring out in modern terms the full force of St. Thomas's argument: "lex naturalis nihil alìud est quam participatio legis aeternae in rationali creatura." The whole emphasis is on the *rationality* of the law of man's behaviour as distinct from the laws of "sub-human physical nature." Man directs his own conduct freely but he is morally obliged to direct it rationally. St. Thomas's natural law moves from the beginning within the sphere of what man *ought* to be and do; but also moves all the time within the sphere of what man *is*.

[31] 1-2, 92, 2 and 3.

[32] Op. cit., p. 75.

[33] Op. cit., p. 129.

[34] P. 65.

[35] The commonest instances of the fallacy to-day are probably to be found in the writings of social psychologists, sexologists and sociologists. To the implied question: "Is such-and-such behaviour normal, i.e. right?" they very commonly answer: "It is normal, i.e. statistically prevalent." This is obviously punning on the two quite different senses of the word "normal": it is equivocation.

[36] We try to illustrate and develop this in our later chapters on sex, love, marriage and parenthood.

3

Christianity and the Flesh

It is a common trait of our scientific humanists that they believe that Christianity "finds something unclean and sinful in the sexual instinct."[37] The historical research on which this charge is based does not seem to go beyond W. E. H. Lecky, *History of European Morals,* London, 1911, vol. II, pp. 109-118, 322 ff., pages eagerly explored by Dr. Glanville Williams, preceded thereto by Bertrand Russell. St. Paul is held to have been the chief author of this morbid "ascetic and anti-sexual" doctrine. St. Paul, according to Russell,

> does not suggest for a moment that there may be any positive good in marriage or that affection between husband and wife may be a beautiful and desirable thing, nor does he take the slightest interest in the family; fornication holds the centre of the stage in his thoughts and the whole of his sexual ethics is arranged with reference to it.[38]

Dr. Glanville Williams, with the fidelity of an

35

echo, repeats that for St. Paul marriage had not "any positive value in human relationships."[39] St. Paul, he thinks, taught, and Christianity still holds, that man is composed of a good principle (the soul or spirit) chained to an evil principle (the body or flesh) and that the body and all its instincts, feelings and pleasures are wicked and must be sternly repressed.

This simpliste version of the doctrine of St. Paul is sufficiently refuted by quoting a few texts.

> Know you not that your bodies are the members of Christ . . . Glorify and bear God in your body.
> I beseech you, therefore, brethren, that you present your bodies a living sacrifice, holy, pleasing unto God, your reasonable service.
> Husbands, love your wives, as Christ also loved the Church and delivered Himself up for it . . . that He might present it to Himself a glorious Church, not having spot or wrinkle or any such thing, but that it should be holy and without blemish. So also ought men to love their wives as their own bodies. He that loveth his wife, loveth himself. For no man ever hated his own flesh but nourisheth and cherisheth it, as Christ also doth the Church . . . Now this is a great sacrament; but I speak in Christ and in the Church.
> The wife hath not power of her own body, but the husband. And in like manner, the

husband also hath not power of his own
body, but the wife.[40]

These last words affirm, for the first time in
history, the equality of the sexes. They are Christianity's categorical rejection of the "double standard" of morality, which Christianity conquered and
which persists where Christianity has not penetrated
or where it has receded.[41]. They are the charter of
feminine emancipation. It is surely in an unguarded
moment that Dr. Glanville Williams puts in a word
of praise of Islam, as being relatively free from
Christian taboos about sex.[42] Is it accidental that
Islam, left to itself, is also relatively free from Christian ideas about the equality of women? One may
surely presume that, as a lawyer, Dr. Glanville
Williams will have heard of what is certainly one of
the great events in the contemporary sociology of
law, the fact that the independent Islamic Republic
of Tunisia adopted, as its Family Code, not the
teachings of the Prophet, but the Christian law of
monogamous marriage.[43]

There is surely no need to refute the allegation
that Christianity is committed to a dualistic view of
man and a Manichean reprobation of the flesh. It
is now taken for granted in all serious discussion
that the Catholic theology and philosophy of the
soul do not involve any Orphic or "Platonic" or
"Cartesian" dualism, any two-substance doctrine,
any ghost-in-the-machine myth.[44] The doctrine of
soul is simply the transcription of the experiential
facts that man is rational in his sensing, intelligent

in his body, spiritual in his sex, a moral person in his instincts. The doctrine of soul is the expression of the truth that man is an absolute value in himself. Our scientific humanists agree in rejecting the notion of soul. The Reverend Mr. Joseph Fletcher writes: "All of this soul-doctrine and soul-oriented morality is a pre-scientific, pre-psychological anthropology."[45] Dr. Glanville Williams, for his part, uses the logical positivist type of jargon (a bit *vieux jeu* nowadays) and calls the soul doctrine metaphysical-mystical, unverifiable, having nothing to do with the empirical facts.[46] The soul could, at most, be "something coming from and returning along a divine dimension which is outside the ken of a biologist."[47]

Our authors, however, enable us to understand what the doctrine of soul means by showing us starkly where its denial leads. The Reverend Mr. Joseph Fletcher heroically concludes:

> Just as we have found that it is necessary to lay aside the notions of natural law and soul because they stand in the way of ethical medical care, so we may find that we have to lay aside the notion of man, about whom so many reactionary, dogmatic and absolute claims are being made.[48]

An interesting confirmation, this, of our claim that the doctrine of the soul is the affirmation of man as an absolute value.

Our authors, in fact, provide us with an answer to the old challenge that the belief in a spiritual and immortal soul is not empirically verifiable. They show us at least how drastic a difference as to the empirical facts there is betwen him who believes and him who does not believe in the existence of soul. He who does not believe in the soul is ready to condone the killing of fetuses, of defective infants, of idiots and mental defectives, of the incurably ill and the useless aged. He who does believe in the soul holds all these acts to be murder and absolutely evil. The difference is one of life and death; it is very verifiable.

37 Dr. Glanville Williams, p. 63. Compare Russell, op. cit., p. 43: "The Christian view that all intercourse outside marriage is immoral was (as we see from St. Paul) based upon the view that all sexual intercourse, even within marriage, is regrettable. A view of this sort . . . can only be regarded by sane people as a morbid aberration. The fact that it is imbedded in Christian ethics has made Christianity, throughout its whole history, a force tending towards mental disorders and unwholesome views of life." Compare Russell's *Why I am not a Christian,* Allen & Unwin, 1957, pp. 20-2, 34, 51-2. Compare the Reverend Mr. Fletcher, op. cit., pp. 78 f.

38 Op. cit., p. 42.

39 P. 57. The Reverend Mr. Fletcher agrees; see p. 78. St. Augustine also gets a bad press from all three.

40 I Cor. 6:15, 20; Rom. 12:1, Eph. 5:25-32; I Cor. 7:4.

41 They make nonsense of Russell's claim that Christianity is committed to a "double standard," invented by males to degrade females (op. cit., pp. 52, 98-9). He says: "It is only with the decay of the notion of sin in modern times that women have begun to regain their freedom" (p. 53)—as is, we suppose, evident in Soho or the Place Pigalle! Russell, however, would retort that "morality has incapacitated (us) from thinking clearly and wholesomely on this topic"; for those are "victims of a sexual obsession" who "harry prostitutes" and "who secure legislation nominally against the

White Slave Traffic, but really against voluntary and decent extra-marital relations" (op. cit., p. 225).

[42] Pp. 54-5.

[43] Decree of 1st January, 1957. See Georges Desmotte in *Famille d'aujourdhui,* Semaines sociales de France, 1957.

[44] See, for example, Jean Mouroux, *The Meaning of Man,* translated by A. H. C. Downes, Sheed & Ward, London, 1948, pp. 41-58; F. Copleston, *Aquinas,* Pelican, 1955, pp. 151-8; Gustav Siewerth, *L'Homme et son Corps,* trad., Plon, Paris, 1957, esp. pp. 138-141; H. Bars, *L'Homme et son Ame,* Grasset, Paris, 1958, pp. 19-112.

[45] Op. cit., p. 218.

[46] Pp. 205-8. Compare Russell, "Mind and Matter," in *Portraits from Memory,* Allen & Unwin, London, 1956, pp. 135-153. It is amusing, though for a critic somewhat frustrating, to find the Reverend Mr. Fletcher, after he has denounced the "soul-doctrine" as an anti-personalist, Manichean dualism (pp. 163 *et al.*), later, when he is distracted by damning the "Natural Law" doctrine, forgetting all this and writing the delightfully Manichean-dualist sentence: "But the body is *it.* It is not a person, nor is it morally competent, necessary though it may be as the basis of human personality. A much better analogy lies in the artist and his materials: man the artist, the body the materials" (p. 212). A devastating refutation of the Reverend Mr. Fletcher's highly "reactionary" dualism can be found in St. Thomas Aquinas, *Summa Theol.,* 1, 76, 1: St. Thomas calls the doctrine *multipliciter vanum*—we might translate: "a nest of tiresome fallacies." It need hardly be said that the Reverend Mr. Fletcher does not believe in the immortality of the soul "as an inherent quality of a human being: this is a pagan doctrine and leads to fearsome prospects of heaven or hell in the life after death" (p. 218).

[47] Op. cit., p. 208.

[48] Ibid., p. 220.

4

Sex and Spirit

In the context of our discussion, the nature of sex and of the human person as a sexual being is clearly central. Indeed, apart from the exigencies of this discussion, philosophical reflection upon the nature of sex is a good starting-point for the study of the complex nature of man. Nothing more clearly than sex shows man's unity-in-duality; for sex is not flesh alone but also spirit. The morality of sex is essentially the safeguarding of its spiritual aspirations, the prevention of the "expense of spirit in a waste of shame."

The scientific humanist expends much time and energy denouncing the Christian notion of sex; but it is hard to find consistency or sense in his own notions about it. At one time we find him speaking of sex as if it were an innocent and harmless source of physical pleasure which may be enjoyed in a spirit of happy frolic whenever the impulse arises.[49] At other times he is speaking of sex as an all-important constituent of character which must not be repressed, physically or mentally, under peril of the stunting and maladjusting of the whole person-

41

ality.[50] At still other times, he is speaking of sex as an overwhelming psycho-physical urge which cannot be resisted anyhow. His use of the playful kitten or the raging tiger metaphor seems to depend on the particular legal reform he is advocating or the particular Catholic moral law he is attacking.

The most common view, however, is that sex is an unmysterious, un-metaphysical, uncomplicated reflex which has been suppressed beneath masses of religious-mystical superstitions, metaphysical mystifications, moral and legal and conventional restrictions and taboos. In order that sex may regain its health and joy, and man his happiness, these irking fetters must be cut away. Sex must be set free. Bertrand Russell concedes that there must be some legal controls in the case of unions in which there are children: "there has to be a social ethic connected with children"; though there should be "as little interference with love as is compatible with the interests of children." Contraceptives of course, ensure that the "interference" of children need not arise; and he holds that "all sex relations which do not involve children should be regarded as a purely private affair."[51] "The older morality," he writes, "has been allowed to poison love . . . Love cannot grow and flourish while it is hedged about with taboos and superstitious terrors, with words of reprobation and silences of horror."[52]

It is a curious backward-looking doctrine, this, of the Rousseauesque man, the noble savage, whom religion and morality, society and civilization have

captured, corrupted and saddened. We find it in
Freud, though it is in him the speculation of an
amateur anthropologist, with no support from his
clinical psychology.[53] It sits oddly on forward-look-
ing, scientific progressives. It would be interesting
to study its historical and philosophical ancestry.
But here we can only briefly consider whether it is
an adequate or convincing account of human sex.

The first thing to notice about it is that it regards sex in man as being essentially, originally, like
sex in animals, an uncomplicated, animal instinct.[54]
But it is a gross error to think of human sexuality
in animal terms. There is nothing in man that is
properly to be called animal.[55] To divide man into
an instinctually-uninhibited animal part and a mor-
ally-and socially-inhibited, civilized, rational part, is
to fall into a modern version of the old Manichean
dualism. Man is one being, though not a simple
being. He is one being, complicated of flesh and
spirit at every level of his nature, in every part of
his experience. His sexual nature is not an animal
part of him. It is informed and infused with his spiritual nature. Sex is never merely physical, biological;
it expresses man's quest for absolutes, his desire for
timeless happiness, for perfect mutual love and
understanding, for unchanging loveableness, for un-
failing faithfulness. The tensions of human love are
not imposed from outside; they are part of its nature, part of its desire for eternity in time, for perfection in a world of imperfection and deception.[56]
The love of man and woman arouses aspirations

which its partners cannot satisfy, makes promises which its partners cannot fulfill. "Woman promises man what God alone can give."[57] Human sex is driven by the divine discontent of man whose heart is too great for fellow-man to fill.

Sex has never been found in history without associations with religion and morality. Sexual love is one of the great revealers of man's need for absolutes and for values. It is one of the profoundest and most moving and disturbing of human experiences, showing man to himself in his loneliness and incompleteness, in his unworthiness and need. It is the source of propagation of human life, satisfying the deep human desire for paternity, touching human existence in its central mystery and wonder and self-interrogation. Small wonder that men could explain sex only by religion, accept sex only as from God, and should demand that sex union be consecrated by divine blessing through religious rites. Religion is not superimposed by history upon sex; men from the beginning experienced sex as sacred; they could not understand it except in a religious setting.[58] The integrating of sex with man's total experience, and therefore also his moral and religious experience, is profound and enduring and, indeed, irrevocable. It is proved to-day by the fact that scientific humanists can hope to change men's sexual *mores* only by abolishing their religion and altering their whole philosophy of man. Sexual behaviour is not an isolable part of human conduct; to change it is not to leave the rest of man's personality and behaviour untouched. A sexual revolution involves a new philosophy of man and the world, of time and of human destiny, of sickness and health, of life and death. The Family Planning experts in India and Puerto Rico, for example, are finding that they can make no appreciable 'progress' because the whole philosophy of life in these societies is opposed to neo-Malthusianism: the experts must begin by effecting a total "change in those attitudes which determine the . . . culture pattern."[59] The works of the scientific humanists are there to prove that man's attitude to contraception determines whether he will think it wrong or right for a mother to kill her defective child, or for a doctor "gently and humanely to extinguish his patient's life."

It is not accidentally that even pagan men use religious language about human love—the language of worship, adoration, immortality, eternity. But it is only about God that this language can properly be used; and the terrible danger of human love is that, unless directed beyond bodies to persons and beyond persons to values and to God, it becomes idolatry and then turns into cynical iconoclasm. Human love desires perfect and paradisal happiness, desires eternity in time. No sexual relationship can fulfil this desire. A love which does not transcend sexual attraction tends inevitably, therefore, to seek from some other partner the ecstasy which this one has failed to give, to seek in some other "perfect moment" the eternity which the first one has not granted.

Love conceived as sexual passion inevitably degenerates into Don Juanism; and Don Juanism is a capitulation of the personality before despotic passion; a flight from time and reality into a spurious, drugged intemporality; an exploitation of others as usable and expendable slaves of Don Juan's monstrous egoism.[60] "Free love" is man enslaved himself to instinct and enslaving others to his passion. "Free love" is unworthy of what man is, inadequate to what man needs. It sees in others "sexual objects," not loved persons; means of gratification, not ends; things, not persons. Sex, isolated from the moral and spiritual, would go, not towards others as persons, but towards "the other sex," ignoring and despising the uniqueness and value of the person of others. "Free love" is sub-personal, subhuman.

There is no theme so prevalent in contemporary literature as that of the sense of futility and triviality, the boredoom and despair, the nausea and disgust which sexual "freedom" has brought to contemporary "emanicpated" youth. They were promised beatitude through the body, and the body has deceived them. Now they turn in cynical, disillusioned routine towards, or in bitter manichean loathing against the flesh that failed. The Reverend Mr. Fletcher thinks that contraceptives will take all sadness out of sex.[61] He should tell that to Jean Paul Sartre or Françoise Sagan.[62] Bertrand Russell is wiser than the Reverend Mr. Fletcher. He writes:

> When people no longer feel any moral bar-
> rier against sexual intercourse on every oc-
> casion when even a trivial impulse inclines
> to it, they get into the habit of dissociating
> sex from serious emotion, and from feelings
> of affection; they may even come to associ-
> ate it with feelings of hatred.

He deplores

> the indiscriminate revolt against all sexual
> morality which has sprung up among con-
> siderable sections of the younger generation;

and warns that

> sex divorced from love is incapable of bring-
> ing any profound satisfaction to instinct.[63]

It is baffling that Russell did not see the incom-
patibility of this with the main theses of his book.
He recognizes that "love is an anarchic force which,
if left free, will not remain within any bounds set
for it by law or custom."[64] Elsewhere he says that
love is "one of the most important things in human
life."[65] How did he fail to see that it follows that
his doctrine of "free love" can derange human
existence, can wreck civilization and lay waste the
world?

Sexual love must go beyond itself or else destroy
itself;[66] it must recognize and realize its moral and
spiritual vocation or else become not animal but
worse than animal. Sex is not something animal,

which can be civilized, humanized. Sex is something human which, if not *kept* human by morality and spirituality, will turn inhuman: and the inhuman is infinitely lower than the animal.[67]

Sex can be true to man, and therefore true to itself, only in the moral and spiritual context which defines man's humanity. Freud talked much about the sublimation of sex; and the word sublimation would seem perfectly chosen to express the ennobling of sex though its submission to moral and spiritual values. But Freud's materialism prejudiced him against explanation of the lower by the higher and in favour of explanation of the higher by the lower. The Freudian use of the term sublimation tends to suggest that the moral and the spiritual are nothing but deflected sexuality. Jean Guitton proposes that we should use instead the word "assumption" for the elevation of sex to the level of the spiritual.[68] St. Thomas Aquinas speaks of the "overflowing" of the spirit over the flesh and the passions;[69] and this well suggests the refreshment and peace which can come to the flesh when and only when man has learned to make sex rest in the home of spirit.[70]

[49] Bertrand Russell's dictum: "Sex is a natural need, like food and drink" (op. cit., p. 226), may be held to typify this attitude. Compare his *Why I am not a Christian,* p. 52 ff. et alibi. But, as we shall see, Russell's philosophy of sex is more complex than this sentence alone would suggest.

[50] Dr. Glanville Williams finds that our Lord's condemnation of adultery, in deed and in thought, is unacceptable. Modern Britain and America would not stand for it. "The

first is not accepted by ordinary opinion in America and Britain: marriage after divorce is not regarded as adultery. The second is impossible as a rule of positive law or conventional morality, and would, if felt deeply as a matter of private conviction, give rise to irrational and unhealthy guilt feelings for transient thoughts that are a perfectly natural expression of sexuality" (pp. 129-130). The Reverend Mr. Fletcher writes: "Many modern psychiatrists warn us against the idea that people should feel just as guilty about bad thoughts as about bad deeds, claiming upon ground of clinical observation that these guilty feelings are pernicious and emotionally destructive. In this connection Dr. Maurice Levine says that this unhealthy habit is based "on the outmoded idea that people can be kept from bad actions by avoiding bad thoughts" . . ."

51 P. 132.

52 Pp. 223 ff.

53 *Civilization and its Discontents,* 1939, pp. 75 ff.; cf. "Thoughts on War and Death" (1915), *Collected Papers* IV, pp. 297-300; "Sexual Morality and Nervousness" (1908), *Collected Papers,* II, pp. 76-99; "Degradation in Erotic Life" (1912), *Collected Papers,* IV, pp. 210-6 Gide had a similar notion, leading to his notorious outbursts: "Famille je vous hais" . . . "Commandements je vois hais."

54 Compare Freud, "Degradation in Erotic Life" cited above, pp. 215-6. It will be seen later that our scientific humanists, who begin by loudly protesting their "personalism" as against Catholic "biologism," in fact end by speaking of human sex and human paternity in the most animal terms.

55 Compare Father Bouyer, *Le Trone de la Sagesse,* Edits. du Cerf, Paris, 1957, p. 116; G. Thibon, *La Crise moderne de l'Amour,* Edits. Universitaires, Paris, 1943, pp. 82-3; Rambaud, "Sexualité et Spiritualité," *Médicine et Sexualité,* coll. "Convergences," Spes, Paris, 1948, pp. 222 ff.; D. von Hildebrand, *In Defence of Purity,* Sheed and Ward, London, 1931, pp. 12-31. See also Jean Guitton, *Essay on human Love* (E. Tr.), Rockliff, London, 1951, pp. 101, 155 ff., A.M. Henry, O.P., *Morale et Vie conjugale,* Edits. du Cerf, Paris, 1957, pp. 126-8.

56 Compare S. de Lestapis, S.J., *Amour et Institution familiale,* Spes, Paris, 1948, pp. 54-5; G. Thibon, *Ce que Dieu a*

uni, Lardanchet, Lyon, 1946, pp. 17, 140-3; Guitton, op. cit., pp. 82-3, 119, 196-7; Dom Aelred Watkin, *The Enemies of Love,* Burns Oates, London, 1958, pp. 18 ff., 80-1.

[57] Gustave Thibon, *Ce que Dieu a uni,* p. 178. This has been translated by A. Gordon Smith and published by Hollis & Carter, 1952, as *What God has joined together.*

[58] See W. Koppers, *Primitive Man and his World Picture,* translated by E. Raybould, Sheed & Ward, London, 1952, pp. 55-62; C. Dawson, "The Patriarchal Family in History," *Dynamics of World History,* Sheed & Ward, London, 1957, pp. 156-166; art. "Mariage," in *Dictionnaire de Théologie Catholique,* col. 2045 ff. Compare D. de Rougement, *L'Amour et l'Occident,* Plon, Paris, 1939, pp. 49 ff.; S. de Lestapis, op. cit., pp. 146 ff., F. Charmot, S.J., *L'Amour humain,* Spes, Paris, 1936, pp. 173 ff.; G. H. Joyce, *Christian Marriage,* Sheed & Ward, London, 1933, pp. 31 ff.

[59] See *The Family in Contemporary Society,* S.P.C.K., London, 1958, pp. 110-119. One authority is quoted as concluding: "Apparently then, materials are not enough, and the neo-Malthusian assumption that, given information, people will act rationally and apply it, would not seem to hold in Puerto Rico." Another significant comment, also a quotation, is: "Many people think that the Chinese, a realistic and not very religious folk, will take easily to this new practice." Gandhi wrote in 1946: "Contraceptives are an insult to womanhood. The difference between a prostitute and a woman who uses contraceptives is solely that the former sells her body to many men, the latter only to one . . ." On another occasion, he wrote: "There always have been and there always will be contraceptive devices; but in the past their use was considered an offence against the Deity. It is the work of our generation to glorify vice by calling it virtue." For references, see S. de Lestapis, *La limitation des naissances,* Spes, Paris, 1958, pp. 44-58.

[60] See S. de Lestapis, *Amour et institution familiale,* pp. 54-5, 58-9, 178-9, with the quotations from Maranon, etc., there given; Guitton, op. cit., pp. 207 ff.; E. de Greeff, *Notre Destinée et nos Instincts,* Plon, Paris, 1954, pp. 164-9; D. de Rougement, op. cit., pp. 201-3, 286-9. Gustave Thibon speaks of: "La tendresse epidermique á coloris purement sexuel que tant de modernes prennent pour l'amour" (op.

cit., p. 101). He points out that the transcendence inherent in sexual love can easily, if love is desacralized, turn into idolatry; and that: "One has never any idol other than oneself; the myth of Narcissus is the only and the eternal symbol of idolatry" (pp. 121-2). Max Picard has underlined the element of escapism, the fragmentation of personality, the option for discontinuity, instantaniety, the flight from God, which are inherent in contemporary eroticism; see *L'Homme de Néant,* trad., Eds. du Seuil, Paris, 1947, pp. 152 ff., *La Fuite devant Dieu,* trad., P.U.F., Paris, 1956, pp. 41 ff.

[61] Op. cit., pp. 98-9 ."There is too much sadness after much human intercourse, and yet much of the tragedy of irrational sexuality could be prevented by the exercise of freedom and responsibility. Contraception provides the way; the sadness of involuntary and unintentional procreation need not come *post coitum* if we want to be men instead of animals" (pp. 98-9). Max Picard speaks of the "destruction of truth," of the advent of the "man of lies" as a necessary preparation for the restoration of the reign of Aphrodite!

[62] The phenomenon is excellently analyzed by Georges Hourdin in *Le Cas Françoise Sagan,* Edits. du Cerf, Paris, 1958.

[63] Op. cit., p. 103.

[64] Ibid. G. K. Chesterton continually and brilliantly expounded the thesis that sex, with its propensities for anarchic violence, can be kept from destroying itself and man only through the laws and institutions of marriage and the family; and that in these institutions sex is not thwarted but liberated and fulfilled. See *What's Wrong with the World;* "On the Institution of the Family" in *Heretics;* "The Sentimentalism of Divorce" in *Fancies versus Fads.* Cardinal Newman wrote: "Quarry the granite rock with razors or moor the vessel with a thread of silk; then may you hope with such keen and delicate instruments as human knowledge and human reason to contend against those giants, the passion and the pride of man." *The Idea of a University,* Longmans, London, 1901, p. 121.

[65] P. 96.

[66] This is magnificently argued by Father L. Bouyer, in *Le Trône de la Sagesse,* chapters V, "Mariage et Virginité," and

VI, "Fecondité de l'Agapé dans la Crucifixion de l'Eros, pp. 109-149.

[67] It has been suggested that Pascal was unfair to the animals when he wrote "Qui veut faire l'ange fera la bête"; but he did not say "will *become* a brute"; but "will *act* the brute"— and this is something only man can do. Man acting the brute is infinitely more terrible and more terrifying than any brute beast.

[68] Op. cit., pp. 175-183. He writes: "Since we are both sensuous and spiritual beings, it is our duty to act as a channel and filter for all that is of the flesh for its assumption into a more lofty and sublime existence. That, without doubt, is the meaning of our destiny" (p. 179). Compare G. Thibon, *Ce que Dieu a uni,* pp. 56-64, 95-6, and *La Crise moderne de l'Amour,* pp. 79-101; A. M. Henry, op. cit., pp. 105-8, 127-132. Max Picard, in *L'Homme du Néant,* declares that since the true mystery and meaning of sex reside in its relation to the spiritual, those who deny the spiritual are driven to explore the ersatz mysteries or mystiques of sexual perversion: plenty of examples are to hand in modern literature from Sade to Jean Genet. Sade said "Virtue can procure only an imaginary happiness. All true joy is in the senses and virtue gives them no thrill." An interesting commentary on Picard's words is provided by Simone de Beauvoir's astonishing defence of Sade in *Privilèges,* Gallimard, Paris, 1955, pp. 11-89.

[69] St. Thomas's terms are *redundat, redundantia.* See *De Veritate,* 25, 5; *Summa Theol.* 1, 81, 3; 1-2, 17, 7; *DeVirtutibus in communi,* 9, 4; *In I Eth.,* 1, 20, Ed. Spiazzi, 239-243. Compare Siewerth, *L'Homme et son Corps,* pp. 125-7.

[70] Jean Guitton speaks of mature love as coming to rest "in a kind of tranquil sacrifice" (op. cit., p. 126). Father Henry speaks of chasity as a happy and firm self-possession in respect of our passions, which, in the case of the married, makes their sexual love more subject to the control of their will and therefore more free, more human and more fulfilling (op. cit., pp. 103-7, 110-120, 126-8). Not the least sign of the trans-animality of human sex is that in man, as contrasted with the animal species, perfect chasity, virginity or complete continence leads to no stunting of development. Leaving aside its supernatural grandeur, perfect chasity pro-

duces an enrichment of the whole personality and realizes, more perfectly than marital chasity, the spiritualizing of the flesh which is the vocation of man. See *Médecine et Mariage,* coll. "Convergences," Spes, Paris, 1952, pp. 11-59; and *Chastity,* coll. "Religious Life," V, Blackfriars, London, 1955, especially Part III, "Psychological and Medical Aspects"; also J. Folliet, "Le Célibat," *Famille d' aujourd'hui,* pp. 251-270.

5

Love and Marriage

"Free love" is a contradiction in terms. As Chesterton said, every man who loves is a tied man, or else a traitor.[71] Even Don Juan has to delude himself, or deceive his present partner, that *this* love is exclusive and for ever. As Gustave Thibon put it, extra-marital lovers speak to one another of "eternity" in order to disguise from themselves or try to legitimate "an impure present."[72] Even the carbon-copy marriages of divorcees repeat the rites and life-long promises of the original; deprived of truth, man must console himself with illusions. Even "free unions" must take on the character of monogamous matrimony,[73] for nothing less and nothing other can satisfy the personality of man or fulfil the expectation which love arouses in the human heart.

Love, loyalty, fidelity are inseparable. Christian marriage has simply taken words from the lips of human love when it says: "I take thee to be my wedded (spouse), to have and to hold from this day forward, for better, for worse, for richer for poorer, in sickness and in health, till death do us part, and thereto I plight thee my troth." Pledge and promises, truth and troth and trust are for ever part of the language of human love.[74] Love of its very nature is directed toward everlastingness. In regard to it, man has only two options: to integrate his life by moral decision in accordance with the exigencies of life-long fidelity, or to let his life slide helplessly into disintegrated adventures; to be master of his life or to be the slave of instinct; to take active control, in freedom, of his human destiny, or to wait passively, fatalistically, for passion to push and pull him where it will.

Nothing is more significant in this connection than the language which Bertrand Russell used in defence of conjugal infidelity:

> There can be no doubt that to close one's mind on marriage against all the *approaches* of love from elsewhere is to diminish *receptivity* and sympathy and the opportunities of valuable human contacts.

> Unless people are restrained by inhibitions or strong moral scruples, it is very unlikely that they will go through life without occasionally having *strong impulses* to adultery . . . Infidelity in such circumstances ought to form no barrier whatever to subsequent happiness, and in fact it does not, where the husband and wife do not consider it necessary to indulge in melodramatic orgies of jealousy. We may go further and say that each party should be able to put up with such *temporary fancies* as are always *liable to occur,*

provided the underlying affection remains intact.[75]

We have *italicized* the signicant words. If ever there was a call to moral cowardice and inertia, it is here. If ever there was a decision to abdicate from decision, it is here. Here is a man giving up control over his own life, letting life drift on a current of impulses which he chooses to call strong because he is himself too weak—or rather, because he has decided to act as if he were too weak—to stand against them. But it is to be noted that, when he has abolished all the commandments governing love, Russell puts a new commandment in their place. So new and strange is it that he has to repeat it again and again.[76] "Married people," he proclaims, "you shall never, in any circumstances, be jealous of your spouses." This Russellian commandment is, however, harder than the whole Decalogue. The Ten Commandments command what is hard, but possible. Russell commands what is impossible because inhuman. The human heart cannot but demand an exclusive love.

Few more mistaken things have been written about human love than Russell's words:

Love can only flourish as long as it is free and spontaneous; it tends to be killed by the thought that it is a duty. To say that it is your duty to love so-and-so is the surest way to cause you to hate him or her.[77]

The truth rather is that genuine love automatically creates a duty because he who loves finds in another person a value which is worthy of the best that he can give to it, and of which he feels that a lifetime will not be long enough for him to strive to make himself worthy[78]. Love is one of man's chief ways of becoming master of his destiny, free of his instinctual impulses. It is one of man's means for "redeeming time" and making it serve its purpose of being our meeting-place with eternity. It is by life-long fidelity that love attains the eternity to which it naturally aspires. Love realizes the true meaning of "the time to come" as the time given us to take in hand the building of our lives; the future it envisages "from this day forward" is a future of moral and spiritual effort.[79] Love is inseparable from morality, for love makes a man go out of himself towards another person, go beyond himself towards a value; and this could stand for the definition of moral duty. Love is the surrender of one's self to the claims of another person on that self. It is submitting oneself to the claims of a value greater than oneself; or rather to the claim of a value which realizes one's greater, truer self. One loses oneself in order to find oneself through and with another.[80]

Love starts with individuals, but creates a community. Love starts with single lives, but demands a shared life, a *married* life. This community, this *married* life, is immediately a source of duty for both partners; it is that shared good thing between them,[81] for the sake of which they will henceforth form a couple, sacrificing two single selves to "Us," thinking, talking, acting not as two "I's" but as "We."[82] In genuine love, two people not merely love each other, but also love their love, and guard it as a priceless thing of which they are not worthy, a thing that has been given to them to keep for one another. "Love," said Saint-Exupéry, "is not two people looking at one another, but two people looking together in the same direction." Bertrand Russell has a persistent nostalgia for a love which will "break down the hard walls of the ego, producing a new being composed of two-in-one"; a love which is "free, generous, unrestrained and wholehearted."[83] But he cannot get beyond the idea that love is something that "happens to" a man. He cannot distinguish love-passion from love-charity, or see that the work of sexual love is an activity of transforming *eros* into *agape*. The ego must laboriously hammer down its own hard walls and *make of itself* a new being. Russell's "free love" is just a refusal to give up one's ego to another so as to form a "We." In it, the self is kept back, reserves its liberty, remains uncommitted, unsure; instead of a community of persons, there is only a provisional arrangement between two suspicious and suspect egoisms; there is only the "co-existence of two solitudes."[84] Russell deplores divorce, especially where there are children. But his marriage-without-commitment is in effect nothing but divorce-without-separation. To borrow words quoted by Thibon, the partners are saying: "Live on in my home with your boredom, and I will resume, at your side, my loneliness."[85]

Russell's notion of love must be exactly reversed: love can flourish only as long as it is dutifully and thoughtfully cared for. Love is not something that is "always liable to occur." It is not something that happens to a man. It is something a man *does*. It is something a man *is*—for the sake of himself, and of another, and of a shared value greater than both. Love is a continuous creation of a higher self; it makes its partners want to *become* better persons.[86] Love of itself implies, involves morality. Love of itself demands and creates laws and institutions. Love of itself postulates indissoluble and monogamous marriage. Its spontaneous declaration is: "I hope in you, and will be such that you can hope in me, always, for the sake of Us."[87] Love, to be truly human, must be a continuous task of turning self-regarding desire into other-regarding charity.[88]

There are tragic cases, where love is betrayed, where there is no longer any attempt at or pretence of a really shared existence. We are not here even attempting to examine the question of divorce, which is not part of our present subject. But just this may be said, that despair is not only a sin against God; it is sin against man. To give up *any* man as "hopeless" is to abandon humanism. It is to treat a man as a thing, an *en-soi;* it is to exclude him from the company of the living; it is symbolically and actually to despair of Man as such. "We must never lose faith in man," says Father de Lubac.[89] We must never lose faith in *any* man: that is harder when it is *this* man, this unfaithful or cruel or drunkard husband; this adulterous or spendthrift or shrewish wife. But, then, is it possible to keep faith to the very end in man, including oneself, without faith in God? The ultimate reason why we can never lose faith in any man is that for God no man is ever *it,* but always *thou;* never a *thing* but always a *person,* for whom it is *never* too late to turn to God and live. There cannot be consistent, integral humanism, without theism. There cannot be successful marriage unless God enters into the community of the couple. In hard cases, when human hope seems lost, the deepest, surest hope, the foundation of all human hope, remains. Its cry is a prayer: "I believe in You for the sake of us." As Gabriel Marcel is always urging, it is not possible to believe, to the very end, in any human *you,* unless one's belief goes always through and beyond him to the Divine *You.*[90]

[71] *What's wrong with the World, Cassell,* London, 1910, p. 50.

[72] Op. cit., p. 148.

[73] Sartre's Mathieu, in *L'Age de Raison,* comes to realize that he has been guilty of bad faith in pretending to despise "bourgeois" marriage, while in effect living what was essentially a "bourgeois-married" life. Compare the remarks of S. de Lestapis in *Amour et institution familiale,* pp. 69-83.

[74] The French point out the common root in *foi, confiance, fiançailles, fiancé.*

[75] Op. cit., pp. 113, 182.

[76] Ibid., pp. 114-5, 182, 188, 246-7.

[77] Ibid., p. 113.

[78] Auguste Comte said: "In the case of two beings so different from one another and so complex as a man and a woman, a whole life-time is not too long for them to know one another properly and to love one another worthily." (Cited by Jean Lacroix in *Force et Faiblesses de la Famille*, Edits. du Seuil, Paris, 1948, p. 46.)

[79] Compare G. Thibon, op. cit., pp. 147-8; A. M. Henry, op. cit., pp. 32-40; see also P. Burgelin, *L'Homme et le Temps*, Aubier, Paris, 1945, pp. 129-131, 136; Jacques Rivière, *De la Sincerité envers Soi-même*, Gallimard, Paris, 1943, pp. 22-36; E. de Greeff, in op. cit., pp. 218 ff., 224; J. Guitton, *L'Existence temporelle*, Aubier, Paris, 1949, pp. 172 ff.

[80] What St. Thomas writes of the love of friendship applies to married love: "When one person loves another, he wishes good to that person as if it were to himself; he feels the other as another 'himself.' That is why a beloved person is called 'another oneself' . . . St. Augustine spoke of the 'half of one's soul' . . . In love of friendship, the lover is in the loved one in the sense that he feels that whatever hurts or helps the other, hurts or helps himself; he treats the will of the other as if it were his own; it is just as though he were in the other, feeling the loved one's pain or pleasure as his own. It is, then, the mark of those who love one another that they want the same things, have the same sorrows, share the same joys." (*Summa Theol.*, 1-2, 28, 1 and 2.)

[81] Claudel, alluding to the sense of an eternal vocation which is inseparable from human love, makes a married pair speak of "that thing between us two which exists from before we were born." (Cited by S. de Lestapis, *Amour et institution familiale*, p. 289).)

[82] See Gabriel Madinier, *Conscience et Amour*, P.U.F., Paris, 1947, pp. 132 ff.; Gabriel Marcel, *Homo Viator*, Aubier, Paris, 1944, pp. 95-132; M. Nédoncelle, *Vers une Philosophie de l'Amour et de la Personne*, Aubier, Paris, 1957, pp. 41-72, 145-155; R. Johann, S.J., *The Meaning of Love*, Chapman, London, 1954, pp. 21-30. See also the papers of G. Madinier and R. Savatier in *Famille d'aujoud'hui*, pp. 185 ff., 271 ff. Compare Lacroix, op. cit., pp. 53 ff., 62-66; S. de Lestapis, *Amour et institution familiale*, pp. 84 ff.,

131 ff. It was said of Sidney and Beatrice Webb that each was much less than half of what the two were together.

83 Op. cit., pp. 99 ff.

84 The words are Sartre's, from *Saint Genet,* Gallimard, Paris, 1952, p. 298.

85 *Ce que Dieu a uni,* p. 128.

86 See Gabriel Marcel's reflections on the theme of *fidelité créatrice,* in *Du Refus à l'Invocation,* Gallimard, Paris, 1940, pp. 192-225; *Homo Viator,* pp. 135-185; *Etre et Avoir,* Aubier, Paris, 1935, pp. 66-80, 137-141. Compare M. Nédoncelle, op. cit., pp. 15-99, and *De La Fidelité,* Aubier, Paris, 1953, passim; G. Thibon, *La Crise moderne de l'Amour,* pp. 9-50. See S. de Lestapis, *Amour,* etc., pp. 64 ff.; Dr. René Biot, *Education de l'Amour,* Plon, Paris, pp. 261-3; Etienne de Greeff, op. cit., pp. 149 ff., 164:9. Professor de Greeff pertinently points out that sex of itself cannot promote value or personality, because it receives its value or disvalue from the moral quality of the personality (loc. cit. and also in *Médecine et Sexualité,* pp. 61-78). Sartre has recently written: "Sexuality is only a way of living, at a certain level and in the perspective of a certain individual adventure, the totality of our human condition." ("Questions de Methode," in *Les Temps modernes,* CXXXX, Sept. 1957, p. 381, reprinted in *Critique de la raison dialectique,* t. I, Gallimard, Paris, 1960: see p. 47). An ill-timed "prophecy" of Russell's illustrates this. He wrote: "The new freedom between young people is, to my mind, wholly a matter for rejoicing and is producing a generation of men without brutality . . . I think also that they are likely to prove less cruel, less brutal and less violent than their seniors" (pp. 124, 129). That was 1929. A generation of young people was soon to be dramatically demonstrating, in war and in peace, the "moralizing" effects of the sexual freedom they had been taught, whether in Britain, America, France or in Nazi Germany. Crimes of sexual violence have never been more numerous than they are in modern "sexually-emancipated" societies.

87 Compare Gabriel Marcel, *Homo Viator,* pp. 81 ff., *Etre et Avoir,* pp. 110-7.

88 Humanism has never produced a delineation of love comparable to St. Paul's: "Love is patient, is kind . . . is not ambitious, seeketh not its own, is not provoked to anger. . . .

beareth all thing, believeth all things, hopeth all things, endureth all things . . . never falleth away" (1 Cor. 13). This is the perfect description of married love in its human aspiration and effort, in its God-directed hope. Compare de Lestapis, *Amour*, etc., pp. 288, ff.; and *La limitation des naissances*, pp. 285-7; J. M. Perrin, O.P., *Christian Perfection and married Life* (E. Tr.), Blackfriars, London, 1958; Dom Aelred Watkin, *The Enemies of Love*, pp. 87-98; Bede Jarrett, O.P., *The House of Gold*, Blackfriars, London, 1954, pp. 68-130; G. Thibon, "La Vie a deux," *Médecine et Mariage*, pp. 237-261; A. Carré, O.P., *Companions for Eternity* (E. Tr.), Blackfriars, London, 1957, pp. 27-8, 43-54; R. Johann, op. cit., pp. 37 ff.

89 *Nouveaux Paradoxes*, Seuil, Paris, 1954, p. 63.

90 *Homo Viator*, p. 81; *Du Refus a l'Invocation*, pp. 183-191.

6

Marriage and Parenthood

"It is marriage alone," says Thibon, "which can satisfy instinct without degrading the person."[91] We have seen that marriage is not an alien yoke imposed on sexuality by culture or religion, but something which grows out of human sexuality itself and answers to its deepest needs. We have seen, too, with Saint-Exupéry, that marriage is not two people finding pleasure in one another, but two people looking together in the same direction. It is two people approaching together towards a value which exists between them but comes from beyond them. It is two people collaborating together in a common life-task. This direction, this value, this life-task, are incarnated in the bearing and rearing of children. From every point of view of a personalist or humanist philosophy, whether we look at the human person psychologically or morally, individually or socially, we find that the sexual love of human persons not merely causes, but expresses a desire for offspring. Human love implores, not only marriage, but fruitful marriage; not only marriage but a family.

The Catholic doctrine on this question is well known but is often misunderstood. It proclaims that the primary end of marriage is the procreation and education of children and that the secondary ends are the growth in mutual love of the spouses and the satisfying of sexual instinct. But it is a gross mistake to think of these ends as if they were isolable from one another, or to speak as if the Church's teaching were "biologistic" or merely reproductive, and regarded the "personalist" aspects of conjugal life as secondary and unimportant.[92] The primary and secondary ends of marriage mutually imply one another. Unless sexual union is such as to be, of itself, open towards the primary end of procreation, then it is not, of itself, complete as physical or as psychical or as spiritual union, and cannot adequately realize the secondary end of a personal relationship either.[93] We are reserving for a later section a full discussion of the arguments brought up in defence of contraception: we do not wish to duplicate that discussion here. At this point, we say only that we hope there to show that all forms of mechanical contraception are varieties of onanism, species of withdrawal. They represent not only physical but also psychical and personal withdrawal. They withhold self-giving. Every contraceptive appliance or device is a "hard wall of the ego" (or of two ego's), refusing to be two-in-one-flesh, refusing to be two-in-one-task.

The contraceptive mentality is, even in a psychological sense, a sign of immature development of personality. Sexuality has an intrinsic urge towards self-giving, self-offering to another; towards self-forgetting and self-transcending in community; towards creating of two the "one flesh" which is the child. Anti-procreative sexual unions represent a "regression" towards infantile and specifically narcissitic sexuality. There is strict psychological justification for speaking of "mutual masturbation."[94] In human personality, the instincts and emotional needs of sex, sympathy, altruism, intimacy, paternity, sociality are inextricably inter-blended. He that would save sex must go beyond it, outside himself, towards other persons, new lives. Sex cultivated for its own pleasure can neither satisfy itself nor fulfil man nor serve society.[95]

Contraception is essentially a refusal of love; for the work of love is paramountly the nurturing of a child. Only in the child is love consummated and two "I's" welded into a "We." Only in their child do a man and woman really love their love and love their marriage and receive unanswerable motive for loving each the other for the sake of "Us."[96] It is in procreating children that a couple realize the deathlessness that is demanded by the very nature of their love: nor just in the sense that their race is reproduced and their name perpetuated; but in the personalist sense that they give eternal value to their life in time by loving into existence the only thing on earth that has eternal value, a human personality. "Loving into existence" a child is not just giving him physical birth but guiding him by love towards the moral maturity in which he himself can meet and make his eternal destiny in time. "Pro-creation" is man's sharing in the work of God, which is directed not just towards producing a life on a date of conception, but towards "making a soul" throughout the duration of man's earthly pilgrimage towards eternity. What mother has not felt with Eve: "I have received a child through God." What father has not felt: "I began to realize what God is only when I became a father."[97]

The "We" that is postulated by human love is not man and wife only, but father, mother and "our" children. This "We," as we have seen, does not "happen," it is jointly created; man and wife must grow into a "We," by unselfish love day by day. This growth into love is prevented where children are voluntarily precluded. The birth of a child is never a biological process. It is the assisting into mature existence of a human person, whose developing personality depends on his parents' love as much as his conception depended on their sexual union and his bodily growth depends on their provision of food and care. There is universal recognition by psychologists and social scientists nowadays of the child's need to be loved. But the child has a deeper need than that of being loved. He needs to be involved in, protected by, rendered secure by, the firm, faithful love his parents have for one another. The child's first claim upon his parents is that they love one another for the sake of "Us-in-our-child." The parents' first duty towards their child is not to love the child, but to love one another around the child. St. Thomas Aquinas called the family the "spiritual womb" of the child;[98] that womb is the parents' indissoluble love. Parents have to go on being fathers and mothers all their lives; and to do so, they must renew their own love for one another all their days.

The primary end of marriage is not procreation alone, but education; and education is, in all senses, a work of love. But the inverse is true, that married love reaches its maturity and realizes its capacity for personal fulfilment only in the rearing of children. We have unexpected support for this whole argument from Bertrand Russell. Russell writes with two personalities in *Marriage and Morals*. It is as though Bertrand were the humanist and Russell were the scientist; and Bertrand were desperately trying to save the humane values and the human love which Russell is determined to destroy; not, however, because he wants to destroy them, but because he is fatalistically convinced that, though man should perish, Science must and anyhow shall go on. He advocates "free love," because "we must be content to let the world go forward rather than back." But he warns that "free love," with its corollary, the elimination of paternity and the abolition of the family, would destroy the most valuable things in human life and entail the disappearance

of civilization. It is a curious kind of love-hate, by
which he seems to let Science seduce him into foreseen disaster; a curious kind of death-wish, by
which he seems to desire and dread the death of
all he loves.

He longs for a love which shall be deep, mature,
life-long;[99] yet he pleads for automatic divorce by
demand, "on the production of a medical certificate
that the wife is not pregnant."[100] He realizes that
where there are children, divorce is a grave injustice
to them, and therefore severely warns:

> While I favour a somewhat lenient law on
> the subject there are, to my mind, so long as
> the bi-parental family persists as the norm,
> strong reasons why custom should be against
> divorce, except in somewhat extreme cases.
> I take this view because I regard marriage
> not primarily as a sexual partnership, but
> above all as an undertaking to co-operate in
> the procreation and rearing of children.[101]

Therefore, in order to have divorce and freedom
for adultery, for "compassionate" or "trial" marriage and for promiscuity, he demands the distinction
of marriage from sexual unions "which do not involve children";[102] and he frequently claims that
freedom for these unions would enrich the personality, especially of youth, would increase human happiness, promote brotherliness and represent moral
progress. And yet, he sternly warns that sexual relations are not love, and that fatal consequences

will follow the divorce of sex from love and the
divorcing of love from parenthood.

    I think that perhaps the chief harm that
would be done to women by the abolition of
the father's place in the home would be the
diminution in the intimacy and seriousness
of their relations with the male sex. Human
beings are so constructed that each sex has
much to learn from the other, but mere sex
relations, even if they are passionate, do not
suffice for these lessons. Co-operation in the
serious business of rearing children, and
companionship through the long years involved, bring about a relation more important and more enriching to both . . . (The
abolition of paternity) would, I believe, im-
mensely diminish the seriousness of men's
relations to women, making them more and
more a matter of mere pleasure, not an intimate union of heart and mind and body. It
would tend towards a certain triviality in all
personal relations . . . The elimination of
paternity as a recognized social relation
would tend to make men's emotional life
trivial and thin, causing in the end a slowly
growing boredom and despair, in which procreation would gradually die out . . .[103]

Pascal said: "Let us take pains to think properly; that is the first principle of morality." No one
reading this mass of what cannot be called less than
irresponsible inconsistencies is likely to think that

Russell passes Pascal's test as a moralist. One must pity the generation which looked or looks to Russell as a moral guide on sexual matters. But at least we have here one of his voices loudly and repeatedly raised to defend the inseparability of sex, love and marriage and the family.

One of Russell's difficulties is that he is haunted, as many contemporaries are, by the Promethean myth as applied to science. As man, in the myth, defied the gods in the beginning and stole fire from heaven in order to be as God upon the earth, so, it is imagined, man has to fight for Science against the old religions, the old metaphysics, the old moralities; and must be content that love and marriage and fatherhood and family should perish, provided that Science shall have all power upon the earth. But they have forgotten one thing; and the late Professor Edouard Le Roy, in his last lectures at the Collège de France, put us in mind of it. The first thing man did with fire was to make a hearth.[104] It is not fire as power but fire as love, fire at the heart of a family, that has made man civilized. Unless Science is made to serve, not abolish, the family it will lead the world fatally forward—into barbarism.

[91] Op. cit., p. 94; compare D. de Rougemant, op. cit., pp. 312 ff.; D. von Hildebrand, *In Defence of Purity,* pp. 89-120.
[92] This is, of course, the constant assumption of our two non-Christian humanists and of their friend, the Reverend Mr. Fletcher. Professor Fred Hoyle goes one better, in *Man and Materialism* (Allen & Unwin, London, 1957, p. 139), by alleging that "voluntary limitation of families is forbidden to Catholics because by so doing the proportion of Catholics to

non-Catholics tends to be steadily increased." Can he explain why the Church condemns contraception among the vast non-Christian populations of India, China, Japan, thus, so far as natural causes go, dooming Catholics to be a steadily diminishing proportion in those populations? The Church pronounces contraception immoral by the natural moral law, binding on all men, whatever their religion. Nobody will ever understand Catholicism, even as a sociological phenomenon, who does not begin by recognizing that the motives of its teaching are religious, not political.

93 Father A. M. Henry brings this out well in his *Morale et Vie conjugale,* pp. 142-9; also in his chapter, "Le Mariage," in *Initiation théologique,* IV, Edits. du Cerf, Paris, 1956: see pp. 754-764. His treatment is, in our view, injured by his persistence in opposing the "morality of charity" to a (quite caricatural) "morality of precepts." The inseparability of the ends of marriage is also evident if we examine the Church's teaching, coming down from St. Augustine, on the three "good things" of marriage: faithful love, fecundity, sacramental grace. See St. Thomas Aquinas, *Summa Theol.,* Suppl., p. 49, and the notes of L. Misserey, O.P., in the volume, *Le Mariage,* I, of the *Somme Théologique* of the Revue des Jeunes, Desclée, Paris, 1930, pp. 205 ff., G. H. Joyce, *Christian Marriage,* pp. 157 ff.; 314 ff.

94 See Dr. Ch. Mertens de Wilmars, *Psycho-pathologie de l'Anti-onception* (Centre d'études Laennec), Lethielleux, Paris, 1955, pp. 32, 65-6, 67-9, 79-91, with the citations from Duyckaerts, Schwartz, Forel, Schockaert, etc., there given. Compare A. M. Henry, *Morale et Vie conjugale,* pp. 154-5; S. de Lestapis, *Amour,* etc., pp. 103-4, also his paper, "La Fecondité," *Famille d'aujourd hui,* pp. 227-250 R. de Guchteneere, *Judgment on Birth Control* (E. Tr.), Sheed & Ward, London, 1931, pp. 148 ff.

95 Professor de Greeff, in a passage already alluded to, writes: "Sex does not develop in isolation, but in close and constant relation with the pre-existing personality . . . Sexual instinct cannot develop towards love, cannot contribute to spiritual progress, unless at its awakening it finds the personality already prepared for this progress. If it is left to itself, and if it is not sublimated by a transformation which links it to the parental instincts, to sympathy, to a social

structure based on love and neighbourliness, sex will not do much to save man; it will not even reproduce the family" (p .227).

96 The desire for a child cannot always be realized; but the mentality of involuntarily sterile couples is totally different from that of voluntarily sterile couples, and their case does not upset our argument. Christian humanism shows the value and the social fecundity of their marriage too. We return to the point later, in dealing with artificial insemination.

97 The words are from a character of Balzac, and are quoted by Jean Lacroix in *Force et faiblesses de la famille,* p. 23. See also S. de Lestapis, *Amour,* etc., pp. 154-165; A. M. Henry, *Morale et Vie conjugale,* pp. 152-3; Lacroix, op. cit., pp. 63-71; Charmot, *L'amour humain,* chapters X, XI, XIII.

98 *Summa Theol.,* 2-2, 10, 12.

99 See op. cit., pp. 96, 99-100, 246.

100 Ibid., p. 185.

101 Ibid., p. 177.

102 Pp. 125-133, 211, 238.

103 Pp. 157, 160. These last words force us to think of Sartreanism. In the whole literary corpus of Sartre there is not a single marriage that is successful, not a single sexual liaison that is fertile (except one, when it leads instantly to plans for abortion), not a single child that is loved, not a single recognition of any value in family life (except the mocking praise of "bourgeois" marriage in *L'Enfance d'un Chef,* which is so grotesque that it fails completely, even as a story). Thibon, though not thinking of Sartre, might have had the Sartrean world precisely in mind when he wrote: "A love which has nothingness for essence, logically refuses to have being for its result." (*Ce que Dieu a uni,* p. 188). Elsewhere, Thibon describes in memorable words the fecundity of generous love: "The meeting of two poverties in love creates wealth; it is enough that two nothings open out to one another for God to be found in their union" (op. cit., p. 168).

7

Is Human Life Sacred?

We have argued that sex is permeated by the human spirit and shares in the sacred value of the human person. Sex is the means of transmission of human life and is thereby the condition *sine qua non* of all human values. Whatever touches the *biological nature* of sex immediately touches the *person and value* of man and the destiny of humanity. We hope to show in succeeding chapters that the new scientific humanist attitude to sex—by which the contemporary world is so much infected—necessarily entrains a new philosophy of man, in which life is no longer inviolable. The modern views of sex and love cannot be lived out without contraceptives, abortion, sterilization, divorce, prostitution, promiscuity; and the modern doctrine of contraception cannot be thought through without endorsing infanticide and the killing of the mentally defective, the incurably sick and the useless old. The neo-Malthusian doctrine of "only wanted babies" involves immediately the doctrine of "unwanted sick and old." We are faced with a philosophy in which no human life is sacred—or safe.

Dr. Glanville Williams calls this kind of consideration the "wedge objection," and he brushes it aside contemptuously as one that has been always used to oppose human progress. Conservatives and reactionaries have always said that any innovation is "the thin end of a wedge." The argument "could be used to condemn any act whatever, because there is no human conduct from which evil cannot be imagined to follow . . ." The Reverend Mr. Fletcher speaks of it petulantly as "a fundamentally obstructionist argument."[105]

Not to encroach on future discussion, we wish here only to say that these writers are both mistaken in thinking that we oppose them with a "wedge-argument." We are not saying, "if some people are allowed do x, others later will go further and do $x+1$. . ." What we are saying is that to approve x is *already* to approve $x+1$ . . . To do x is already implicitly to do $x+1$ . . .; because to do x is to will the principle which is involved in doing $x+1$ . . .; to approve x is to adopt a philosophy which admits of no reason why $x+1$ . . . should not be done.[106] What we contend is that to approve of the principle of contraception is to accept a philosophy of human life which leaves one with no reason for regarding any human life as invioable. Humanism entails giving up the notion that man as such has an absolute value.

The detailed proof of this will follow. Meanwhile we merely quote some of the starker of the passages in which our humanists state the exceptions, the conditions, the qualifications (even educational and social!) which must be granted before they are prepared to concede that a human life is valuable or inviolable.

The Reverend Mr. Fletcher (speaking of euthanasia), says:

> Our courts already recognize and allow what they call justifiable homicide in some circumstances when we are attacked by other human beings. What the lawyers have not explained to the satisfaction of many interested moralists is why the same ethical elasticity may not be applied in cases of attack by disease and incurable suffering . . . If it is replied that in self-defence against human attack we are seeking to preserve our life, whereas in euthanasia we are seeking to detroy our life, then we can and must call into question any such pure vitalism. We must deny that "life" is adequately understood as mere vital existence or breathing! For the man of moral integrity and spiritual purpose, the mere fact of being alive is not as important as the terms of the living . . .
> Sometimes we hear it said that the moral and legal approval of euthanasia would weaken our moral fibre, tend to encourage us to minimize the importance of life . . .
> It is very hard to find any real hope of tak-

ing hold of an objection like this, with its broad value-terms such as "moral fibre" and the "importance of life."[107]

Dr. Glanville Williams (speaking of euthanasia), says:

It is good that men should feel a horror of taking human life, but in a rational judgment the quality of the life must be considered . . .[108]

There is another context in which Dr. Glanville Williams expresses views about the "quality" of life; it is when he is discussing "Contraception and Eugenics"; and the juxtaposing of the two contexts is an interesting exercise. "Quality of life" is found to have a surprising correlation with "quantity of salary." We quote:

There is, in addition, the problem of eugenic quality. We now have a large body of evidence that, since industrialization, the *upper stratum* of society fails to replace itself, while the population as a whole is increased by excess births among the *lower and uneducated classes* . . . It is impossible to be satisfied with a state of affairs in which tomorrow's citizen are produced and brought up, in disproportionate numbers, by the *under-educated and poverty-stricken* groups . . . This differential fertility between different classes is largely if not entirely due to the fact that the *well-off and intelligent* make use of contraception, while those of low socio-economic status do not do so on the same scale . . .[109]

The italics are ours; they provide interesting points for reflection on humanism and its relations with democracy. There is no need to say more at this point. We have quoted enough to make thinking men pray that God may preserve humanity from the humanists.

Gabriel Madinier has said that one of the indispensable services the family renders to mankind is to remind man that he can save himself only in and through human nature.[110] The family teaches man the human means to the improvement of man: love, patience, persuasion, education, moral endeavour, hope, prayer. The family believes in man. It teaches us that we can never despair of any man. But scientific materialism despairs of improving man by human means. It substitutes force for persuasion, power for love, techniques for moral effort. It tells man, not to improve himself, but to wait for scientific "straighteners" to improve him. It despises man, the ordinary man, the dull and stupid man, the weak and sickly man, the senile and useless man, the "poor stock," the "unfit members," the "mentally and physically ill-equipped," "the lower and uneducated classes."[111] The humanist cannot live with men as they are. Humanism cannot tolerate men as they are. It wants to manufacture something better. But this sort of humanism cannot create; it can only destroy. All the chapters of Dr. Glanville Williams's book have to do with the Destruction of Life.[112] Dr. Glanville Williams has, however, taught us much. Not least, he has taught us what a scientific humanist is. He is one who believes in Science but does not believe in man.

[104] E. Le Roy, *Essai d'une Philosophie première,* I, *La Pensée,* P.U.F., Paris, 1956, p. 439.

[105] P. 198.

[106] This line of thought obviously rejoins the truth of Kant's reasoning in the first form of the Categorical Imperative. It is philosophically very naive to speak of this as a "wedge argument."

[107] Op. cit., pp. 186-7, 201. We quoted earlier a passage in which he suggests that, in the interests of "ethical medical care," we may have to "lay aside the notion of man about whom so many reactionary, dogmatic and absolute claims are being made" (op. cit., p. 220).

[108] P. 281.

[109] Pp. 73, 74.

[110] Quoted by Jean Lacroix, *Force et faiblesses . . .,* p. 73.

[111] Quotation marks indicate phrases from Dr. Glanville Williams.

[112] Except one, which has to do with the destruction of fatherhood, or the production of human life by sub-human means.

8

Contraception

Nothing is so conspicuous in the literature of contraception as the shabbiness of the arguments used to give it moral justification. This alone should lead intelligent people to suspect the practice: that behaviour could not be honourable which needs to invoke such fraudulent reasoning. Indeed from the Bradlaugh-Besant trial in 1877 until, and including, the Lambeth Conference of 1958, there has been no solid argument of a philosophical, moral or religious character in favour of artificial contraception. What there has been is emotive advocacy, "persuasive" redefinition of terms and the other tricks so familiar to us as the stock in trade of the advertiser and propagandist. A recent writer on Propaganda has stressed its reliance on emphatic assertion, not argument, on emotion, not reason; on its use of "double-talk words" or "words which are more important as words of praise or blame than as words of precise description." The main ingredients of modern advertising he finds to be the emotions of sex appeal, snob appeal or the desire to buy and do what "the best people" buy and do, fear and greed.[113] He

81

could have found all his illustrations both of propaganda and of advertising in the writings of the contraceptionists. Some of the most perfect examples are to hand in the books of Dr. Glanville Williams and the Reverend Mr. Fletcher.

The latter's chapter on this subject is solely an effort to create, by emphatic and repeated assertion, favourable emotional, moral and religious associations or pro-attitudes with the notion of contraception. The chapter is sub-titled: "Our right to control parenthood." The struggle" for contraception is said to be part of the stubborn advance of mankind, onward and upward, towards moral maturity; part of the emancipation of woman from "helpless fecundity"; part of our "march to moral stature in parenthood"; part of "man's inherent drive to climb the ladder of self-determination and self-understanding." A sub-section is headed, by the Reverend Professor, "Religion and Repression." Science, however, he claims, gives deliverance to the captives of religion, makes parenthood and birth "matters of moral responsibility, of intelligent choice." "Sex is no longer," thanks to science, "a helpless submission to biological consequences"; science makes us "persons and not merely bodies," "takes the accident out of parenthood," makes us "men instead of animals."[114]

We are bound to point out that the Reverend Mr. Fletcher flatly contradicts himself when, in a later chapter, he is advocating Artificial Insemination. On page 71, he is perturbed about world (and

American) over-population; while on page 140 he is worried that, with the illegitimate birth-rate going down and sterility increasing, a point must come "at which there will be fewer children available for adoption than would-be parents wanting them." For this reason, the pressure for Artificial Insemination by Donors will certainly increase. "Not many couples will be content with a permanently barren love." He has by now forgotten also his pious horror of biology; he argues, in favour of A.I.D., that "the end or purpose of parenthood is implanted in us biologically and emotionally . . ." He pleads that A.I.D. is not adultery, because adultery is "personalist," while A.I.D. is purely impersonal, physiological, biological.[115] Such inconsistencies betray the utter weakness of the scientific humanist case.

One may wonder, also, why, if contraception is so self-evidently morally good and even morally superior as its advocates pretend, it should be necessary to provide the public with so much reassurance of its moral innocence. Is it that conscience is still hard to convince, or at least to still? One wonders, for example, why the propagandists should be so careful to associate contraception with science. It is not immediately evident what science has to do with the most widely used forms of contraception. Contraceptive methods, of one sort or another, are as old as man.[116] However, Dr. Glanville Williams, who makes this point, himself observes, "all this does not prove that birth control is right, because savages do many wrong things."[117] Science, however, unlike the savage, is both modern and civilized and good; and that is why it is effective to associate it with a desired end, like contraception. The word is put in for emotional reassurance; it is a conscience-tranquilizer.

Much of the literature on contraception is, we maintain, salesmanship or propaganda, mobilizing the emotions and deploying the prestige-symbols and "selling emotional security and ego-gratification" like the "Hidden Persuaders."[118] The following passage from a recent popular book illustrates the genre perfectly, with its skilfully blended appeals to fear, ambition, snobbery, self-respect, moral superiority-feeling, reassurance of worth.

> No woman can afford to be ignorant of modern contraceptive appliances if she is to lead a civilized life. The price of this ignorance is tragedy multiplied by tragedy . . . Civilized human beings have children when they desire them, not accidentally, as a result of wild and irresponsible sexual congress . . . Hence the importance of contraceptive knowledge to every adult human being.[119]

Someone has said that, in this age of the Art of Selling, we need to cultivate the Art of not Being Sold To. For this, nothing is required except to think before you buy. Not much thinking about these sentences is required in order to see that the words do not truthfully describe the realities in question. They suggest that to practise contraception is to be continent; not to practise contraception is to be incontinent; whereas contraception is precisely the pronouncing of continence as impossible. It is long since Chesterton protested against the "quaint" title, "Birth Control, which is in fact "a scheme for preventing birth in order to escape control."

There are no phrases that recur more often in the writings of contraceptionists than the phrases, "wanted babies," voluntary parenthood."[120] Like the related phrases "planned parenthood" and "planned family," these are guilt-assuaging and moral-satisfaction-suggesting stimuli. It is important to realize just what is being done by the use of these phrases. They are being "persuasively re-defined"; that is to say, the usual *meaning* of the phrases is being subtly changed so that the moral and emotional approval elicited by the *words* may be attached to a new form of behaviour which it is desired to recommend. As the phrases are now used, they permit only habitual contraceptive-users to be called "voluntary parents"; and only the babies and families of habitual contraceptive-users to be called "wanted babies" or "planned families." All the pregnancies of non-contraceptive-using parents are by definition "accidental pregnancies" and all their babies are by definition "unwanted babies." In other words, "wanted babies" are the babies of those who throughout their married lives habitually do not want babies and who ensure, by regular use of contraceptives, that they do not have them; but who, on a carefully restricted number of occasions cease to "unwant" babies and suspend temporarily the use of contraceptives.[121]

But the terms "wanted babies" or "planned pregnancies" need to be more deeply analyzed. Surely they represent a union of incompatibles. They suggest that wanting a baby is like wanting a new car; that planning its birth is like planning a factory. But the whole of the spontaneous language of parents shows that these strings are false. A couple 'expect' the 'arrival' and the 'company' of their baby as one expects the arrival from abroad of a loved relative one has never met; as one awaits the company of someone unknown and yet familiar. A pregnancy is a hopeful readiness to receive, not a planned operation; it is an attitude of prayer, not an exercise of power.[122] It is a personal encounter with the unknown, a journey into mystery, not an engineering project.[123] A baby is a gift, not a product. The mother 'presents' 'their' child to the father; it is the most mysterious and wonderful gift she ever gave, or they ever received. The baby is 'given to,' 'born to' his parents. He is their son, yet not their property; something in him does not belong to them; in his personality he stands apart from them and holds from them, from infancy, a secret of future character and liberty and destiny which they cannot predict or control.[124] They can only, in love and hope, help him to be *another* self. "Wanting" a child, like loving him, or one's spouse around and about him, is not the emotion of a day but the vocation of a life. A child is welcomed, not just "wanted," and must be welcomed all through life. Mother love, like marital love, is what a woman does and is. Like everything human, it is precarious and constantly in danger from the all-too-human in ourselves. It must be humbly tended and persever-ingly renewed. "Wanted babies" and "planned fam-ilies" are the result of the moral and spiritual ma-turing of married persons, not of automatic and mechanical techniques. The sphere of sex and pro-creation is the sphere of the sacred, the mysterious, the personal; and the intrusion into it of the con-cepts of mechanics is the beginning of a process of dehumanization which cannot but spread over the whole of human life.[125]

Dr. Glanville Williams has little that is new to say on the subject of "the control of conception." He shares the fear of world over-population, which is sincerely felt by many of our contemporaries, and which seems indeed to be one of the few remaining cosmic anxieties of a generation of intellectuals who profess themselves untouched by metaphysical or religious disquiet. No one will deny that there is a problem; but there is no justification for a panic. One frequently has the impression that opinions on this question reflect rather the philosophy of the speaker than the objective facts.[126]

The most recent survey, that carried out by the United Nations' Department of Economic and Social Affairs, on *The Future Growth of World Population*,[127] is significantly restrained in tone.

Although obviously perturbed at the extent and especially the rapidity of world population growth, and at the consequent critical shortage of time for making the necessary global adjustments, the Report says:

> (At what point would the earth reach its maximum carrying capacity?) . . . Despite many attempts to find an answer to this question, the problem cannot be solved by scientific reasoning. Because of his powers of reflection, man adapts himself to ever changing circumstances, and his eventual adjustment to a new situation cannot be predicted before that situation has risen. Different technical and organisational responses to a given environment evidentally will permit different numbers of human beings to exist on earth . . . In view of current scientific progress, conditional estimates of the world's population-carrying capacity may now have to be revised upwards. Recently our attention has been drawn to vast unused resources of vegetable substance in the sea, the possible uses of solar energy, and the likelihood that atomic energy will become widely available as a source of power in the near future. Other scientific discoveries may yield surprising results in terms of a more intensive use of the gifts of nature. But it is doubtful whether the limit to human numbers depends on technological progress alone

. . . Not only technical achievement but progress in international co-operation and organization will have to be more effective than during the past 43 years if the expected numbers of mankind are to be organizationally and technologically accommodated to the minimum conditions required for human dignity.[128]

In other words, the world-population problem is a challenge to be met by intellectual, moral and spiritual greatness; it calls for the building of a new one world of charity, peace and humanized science, economics and technology. Christians will co-operate with all men of good will to meet the challenge by all means that are morally good. What they will never do is to call evil good, or do an evil thing in the hope of securing good effects. And in this determination, they will be sure that the good effects are only apparent and that the total fruit of an evil sowing must itself be evil. They will know, in the words of the distinguished Ulster Protestant gynaecologist, Dame Louise M'Ilroy, that "what is morally wrong cannot be scientifically right" and that "anything which interferes with natural laws is bound to have repercussions on those who break them."[129]

The British Royal Commission on Population, although endorsing Birth Control ideology, rather incongruously warned:

There is much to be said for the view that a failure of a society to reproduce itself indicates something wrong in its attitude to life which is likely to involve other forms of decadence. The cult of childlessness and the vogue of the one-child family were symptoms of something profoundly unsatisfactory in the *Zeitgeist* of the inter-war period, which it may not be fanciful to connect with the sophistication and complacencies which contributed to the catastrophe of the second world war.[130]

We may recall that Péguy said: "Nobody ever works except for children." The Commission urged a "replacement size of family" for Great Britain, which would require "a decided increase in the proportion of families with three or four children."[131] These parts of the Commission's findings have seldom been repeated by scientific humanists when discussing population problems.

Dr. Glanville Williams and the rest of them urge that the reduction in the death rate and the prolongation of life expectation by improved medicine entail as a corollary the proportional reduction of births so as to ensure a stable population: death control, they assert, involves birth control. The argument is specious but simpliste. Again, the Royal Commission was more scientific when it stressed the importance of population balance as distinct from population stability. "Death control," mathematically offset by "birth control," entails a gradually senescent society with all the economic, social, political and moral consequences of geron-

tocracy.[132] The Commission notes the economic
and other advantages of an expanding population.
It concludes:

> It thus seems possible that a society in which
> the proportion of young people is diminish-
> ing will become dangerously unprogressive,
> falling behind other communities not only in
> technical efficiency and economic welfare,
> but in intellectual and artistic achievement
> as well.[133]

The logical "fall of the land" is, unfortunately,
the opposite to that suggested: it is birth control
policy which logically entails "death control," and
that in the quite brutal sense of planned infanticide
and legalised euthanasia. Dr. Glanville Williams as
usual obliges by showing where the logic can lead:
"It may, indeed, be," he says, "that mankind will
one day have to revise its present ethics of keeping
people alive."[134]

Meanwhile, in the interval before scientific humanism gets as 'tough' in practice as it now is in
proposal, we can ponder some of the criteria on
which it may one day be decided who may be "kept
alive" and who may not. To begin with, we are told
by Dr. Glanville Williams that "backward countries" should not receive financial aid from the
United States or Great Britain unless these countries accept "provision for the reduction of fertility." The Colombo Plan for South-East Asia and
the Anglo-American proposal to finance the High
Aswan Dam in Egypt are condemned for omitting

this proviso. (History has had the last laugh on this particular paragraph.) This is not the first time that proposals have been made for Malthusian strings to sterling—or dollar-aid bags.[135] Those who make them might ask themselves whether the West's failure even to impress or be respected by, much more to lead, the East, may be due to its own moral and spiritual failure at home. This failure has global repercussions. As Birth Control propagandists in the West repeat their hackneyed lines, *the* world demographic problem appears in its stark reality as the question: Can Western man retain his civilizing influence in world history? As the United Nations' Report estimates:

> The technologically advanced areas contain now slightly more than one-third of the world population. This share, according to the seemingly most plausible expectations, will drop to less than one-quarter by the end of the century . . . but it may also dwindle to one-fifth.[136]

Bertrand Russell has long envisaged the "dying out" of "the most intelligent classes in the most scientific nations," and the decline of the white man's influence, as the inevitable result of birth control, which, nevertheless, he never ceases to advocate.[137] For 'scientific' and 'technological' in these passages, we would substitute 'Christian,' fully conscious that there is no identification between Christianity and the West, yet recognizing that as the West has had special privilege from, so it has also special responsibility toward Christianity. From this point of view, to mention no other, it is evident that birth control and its sequelae are perhaps the gravest betrayal of Christianity ever perpetrated by Christian people.

Pursuing this search for hints of the shape of a scientific humanist future, we find Dr. Glanville Williams gravely disturbed by the fact that "tomorrow's citizens are produced and brought up, in disproportionate numbers, by the under-educated and poverty-stricken groups"; while the "well-off and intelligent"[138] inevitably decline. "At the same time," he complains, "Britain operates a family allowance scheme which gives an incentive to produce children only to the poorest orders of society." (We have already called attention to the interesting correlation of intelligence and virtue with class and income.) Like Bertrand Russell, he expects "the pressure of democratic opinion," with its unscientific assumption that men are equal, to be an obstacle to "a rational policy to correct dysgenic tendencies."[139] Birth Control has its politics too, and they point forward—to "1984."

One final argument of Dr. Glanville Williams in favour of contraception is that it "greatly reduces the crude and wasteful method of family limitation —abortion and infanticide—that tend to be otherwise resorted to."[140] This is just not true; and Dr. Glanville Williams knows it. Only thirty pages later, he is arguing that the

limitation upon the effectiveness of contra-

ception . . . creates the need for both sterilization and abortion as subsidiary means of
family planning and of eugenic and population control. Abortion, though sometimes
the only possible solution, is a costly and
wasteful form of birth control . . . (But)
sterilization settles the problem once and for
all.[141]

He knows the evidence that in Japan, Sweden
and Denmark, where contraception is official policy
and abortion is legalized, illegal abortion has increased steadily as contraception became more general and legal abortion more frequent.[142] Let us note
also that the increase in all forms of sexual sin is
not coincidental but an inevitable result of contraception. Birth control habits develop the determination not to have children at any cost; if "by accident" a pregnancy has not been successfully prevented, there will be an inevitable readiness to ter-
minate it by any means. Birth control *mores* create
a mentality of "unwanting" babies. Furthermore, it
is not a practice only but a new philosophy of man
and sex, a new "way of life."[143] It means the abandonment of self-control over sexual urges; it implicitly authorizes sexual promiscuity.[144] The real
problem of our time is that society tolerates a continuous and ubiquitous display, by every medium
of mass communication, of artificial libidinous so-
licitation, which makes it unnaturally difficult for
people, particularly young people, to be continent;
and then offers a remedy, contraceptives, which

merely increases the incontinence. Promiscuity is
the logic of birth control; but to have promiscuity
with impunity there must also be abortion and infanticide, sterilization and euthanasia. The logical
contraceptionist must insist that if these cannot be
generalized by persuasion, they must be imposed by
law. It has long been recognized that there is a connection between eroticism and totalitarianism.[145]

[113] Lindley Frazer, *Propaganda*, Home University Library,
1957. Professor Fraser Brockington, in his recent Penguin
on *World Health* (1958), discussing population-control policy, disfavours sterilization and abortion, prefers "control
of the family by contraceptive techniques." He has these
significant remarks: "This can be taught as part of the ma-
ternity and child welfare movement, and in marriage guid-
ance . . . and awareness can be aroused through intensive
health education of the public. The modification of public
attitudes may be slow, but there are means at our disposal,
including wireless and television . . . Moreover we have
reached a better understanding of how to further social
movements through small groups and organisations" (p.
106). He is Professor of Social and Preventive Medicine at
Manchester University.
[114] Op. cit., pp. 65-99.
[115] Op. cit., pp. 121, 129 et saepe.
[116] See the Reverend Mr. Fletcher in op. cit., p. 68; Oswald
Schwartz, *The Psychology of Sex*, Penguin Books, 1951,
pp. 9-10.
[117] Op. cit., p. 54.
[118] See *The Hidden Persuaders*, by Vance Packard, Longmans, London, 1957, p. 67.
[119] W. Beran Wolfe, *How to be Happy though Human*, Penguin Books, 1957, pp. 305-6. He goes on to characterize non-
contraceptive societies as militaristic and masculine-domi-
nant; whereas "in a country that depends for its security on
the happiness of its inhabitants and on international co-
operation and peace, whose population is one of choice,
conceived in love and nurtured in responsibility, the limita-

tion of offspring by the conscious control of conception is as self-understood and self-explanatory as plague control and public hygiene."

[120] Generous use was made of them by the British *Royal Commission on Population Report,* 1949 (Cmmd. 7695). See especially paras. 427-8. "We agree with the view that there is nothing inherently wrong in the use of mechanical methods of contraception . . . The spread of contraceptive knowledge represents a big extension of man's control over his circumstances . . . It has made possible for increasing numbers of people the planning of the size of their families, and has helped to free women from excessive burdens and to ensure that more and more of the children born are wanted children. Control by men and women over the numbers of their children is one of the first conditions of their own and the community's welfare, and in our view mechanical and chemical methods of contraception have to be accepted as part of the modern means, however imperfect, by which it can be exercised. We contemplate therefore that, with the spread of effective knowledge of contraception, voluntary parenthood will become more or less universal."

[121] In Birth Control Ethics contraceptive intercourse is the rule, natural intercourse the calculated exception. Cf. O. Schwartz, op. cit., p. 19: "By using contraceptives and dispensing with them only when a child is honestly desired, we replace a haphazard happening by a resolve of our free will." In other words, Birth Control doctrine proposes, not just an occasional variation in marital practice, but a radically new concept of marital relations and indeed of marriage.

[122] In Ireland, a pregnant woman is sometimes said to be in 'a blessed condition.'

[123] Compare Schwartz, op. cit., p. 30: "Sex . . . cannot be treated in a perfectly 'natural' manner because it is more than a purely 'natural' phenomenon. For human sexuality is shrouded in mystery . . . the essential mystery which surrounds our origin: the mystery of origin, companion to the mystery of death, the Unknown from whence we came, and the Unkonwn to which we go."

[124] Compare the words of a mother, quoted by S. de Lestapis in *Amour et Institution Familiale,* Spes, Paris, 1948, pp.

135-9; cf. Lacroix, *Force et Faiblesses de la Famille,* Edits. du Seuil, Paris, 1950, pp. 58-9, 69-71.

[125] Compare Jean Guitton, *Essay on Human Love,* E. Trans., Rockliff, London, 1951, pp. 206-7.

[126] For example, Professor Fred Hoyle paints a macabre picture, which really turns into the grotesque, in *Man and Materialism,* Allen & Unwin, 1957, pp. 122-140; compare his *Decade of Decision,* Heinemann, London, 1955, pp. 99-103. Contrast S. de Lestapis in *Famille d'Aujourd'hui,* Sémaines Sociales de France, 1957, pp. 229 ff. 239-240.

[127] *United States Population Studies,* No. 28, New York, 1958.

[128] Op. cit., pp. 21-2. Compare the *Royal Commission on Population Report,* para. 361: "It is desirable to appreciate the dangers of using a narrowly utilitarian calculus to determine issues of population policy." Professor Colin Clark's views on this subject are well known. He estimates that, with present agircultural techniques, the world could give European standards of food to 28,000 million people, or ten times its present population. With perfectly feasible improvements of technique, the world could feed thirty times its present population. He writes: "The material resources of the world would easily suffice (to provide a satisfactory livelihood) not only for the whole human race as it now is, but for any conceivable expansion of our numbers which is likely to occur for a very long time. Whatever was the case in the past, we can certainly say now that with modern science and technical knowledge, the fact that so many people fall short of a satisfactory livelihood must be blamed entirely on human shortcomings and not upon the inadequacies of nature." (*World Justice,* I, Louvain, Sept., 1959, p. 35). Professor Clark is Director of the Agricultural Economics Research Institute at Oxford. On the subject of world population, see further: S. Lestapis, *La limitation des naissances,* Spes, Paris, 1958; *Chronique Souale de France,* No. 5, 1953, "Malthus a-t-il été prophète?"; L.-J. Lebret, *Suicide ou survie de l'occident?,* Les éditions ouvrierès, Paris, 1958; J. Vialatoux, *Le peuplement human,* t. I. *Faits et questions;* t. II. *Doctrines et théories,* Les éditions ouvrierès, Paris, 1957; J.-P. Dubois-Dumée, *Va-t-on controler les naissances,* Paris, 1956.

[129] Cited by A. Bonnar, *The Catholic Doctor* (6th edition), Burns Oates, London, 1952, p. 70.

[130] Op. cit., para. 362.

[131] Op. cit., paras. 363, 421.

[132] For example, the Commission remarks: "The charges falling on the budget for the relief of old age will increase over the next generation to an extent which would startle the public if it were generally appreciated" (para. 257). Compare the whole of Chapter XI on "The Age Balance."

[133] Para. 321.

[134] Op. cit., p. 310.

[135] It was made, for example, by William Vogt, in *Road to Survival,* Gollancz, London, 1949.

[136] Op. cit., p. 23; cf. p. 29.

[137] See *The Scientific Outlook* (Third Impression), Allen & Unwin, London, 1954, p. 245.

[138] "Intelligent," in contraceptionist propaganda, obviously includes in its definition, "contraceptive-using."

[139] Op. cit., pp. 73-6; cf. p. 83. The thought of eugenists has not changed since Charles Darwin, in *The Descent of Man* (1871), wrote: "The very poor and reckless, who are often degraded by vice . . . tend to increase at a quicker rate than the provident and generally virtuous members. Or as Mr. Grey puts the case: 'The reckless, squalid, unaspiring Irishman multiplies like rabbits; the frugal, foreseeing, self-respecting, ambitious Scot, stern in his morality, spiritual in his faith, sagacious and disciplined in his intelligence, passes his best years in struggle and in celibacy, marries late and leaves few behind him. Given a land originally peopled by a thousand Saxons and a thousands Celts—and in a dozen generations five-sixths of the population would be Celts, but five-sixths of the property, of the power, of the intellect, would belong to the one-sixth of Saxons that remained. In the eternal 'struggle for existence,' it would be the inferior and *less* favoured race that had prevailed—and prevailed by virtue not of its good qualities but of its faults.' . . ." (Edition published by John Murray, London, 1901, pp. 212-3.) Like our contemporary "scientific humanists," Darwin, following W. R. Grey, A. R. Wallace and F. Galton, already favoured a 'stud-farm' approach to human reproduction: "The weak members of civilised societies propagate

their kind. No one who has attended to the breeding of domestic animals will doubt that this must be highly injurious to the race of man. It is surprising how soon a want of care, or care wrongly directed, leads to the degeneration of a domestic race; but excepting in the case of man himself hardly anyone is so ignorant as to allow his worst animals to breed" (op. cit., p. 206). Compare n. 12 to p. 140, op. cit., p. 53. Compare our pp. 12-14 supra.

[140] Op. cit., p. 53.

[141] Op. cit., p. 82.

[142] Op. cit., pp. 214-233. See also S. de Lestapis in *Famille d'Aujourd'hui,* p. 233-7; *La limitation des naissances,* pp. 59, 66; Guchteneere, *Judgement on Birth Control,* Sheed & Ward, London, 1938, pp. 180 ff., Leclercq, *Marriage and the Family,* E. Trans., Pustet, New York, 1947, pp. 272 ff., A. M. Henry, *Morale et Vie Conjugale,* Cerf, Paris, 1957, pp. 175-6. The vaunted population-control of Japan, claimed as a success for contraception, is in fact effected primarily by abortion, and that on an appalling scale. Legal abortions in Japan number nearly 1¼ millions per annum, and the actual number of abortions is reckoned by the Japanese Welfare Ministry to be twice that number, or above 2¼ millions per annum—which is more than the annual number of births (less than 2 millions). In addition, sterilizations total about 40,000 annually (officially; actually there are estimated to be perhaps ten times that number). This is despite the most vigorously organized, state-promoted contraceptive campaign in the world or in history—giving the Japanese people, for example, one official contraceptive adviser per 3,000 people. See A. Zimmerman, *Overpopulation,* Catholic University of American Press, Washington, 1957, pp. 60-6; S. de Lestapis, op. cit., pp. 293-6. American surveys indicate that abortions are from four to ten times more frequent among contraceptors' than among 'noncontraceptors'; and it is estimated that "the abortionists can thank birth-controllers for 75 per cent. of their business"; see Mihanovitch, Schnepp & Thomas, *Marriage and the Family,* Bruce, Milwaukee, 1954, pp. 364-5.

[143] Russell rightly said: (for those who use them) . . . "contraceptives have altered the whole aspect of sex and marriage." *Marriage and Morals,* p. 133.

144 Dr. Glanville Williams writes: "The refusal of advice to unmarried women is a typical instance of the unimaginative moral outlook which fears that the giving of contraceptive advice will encourage immorality. In fact, if an unmarried woman comes for such advice without reference to marriage, the only probable consequence of refusal is that a child will be born with all the disadvantages of illegitimacy" (op. cit., p. 50). He has obviously strange ideas about what constitutes "immorality."

145 Compare Bertrand Russell, *The Scientific Outlook,* pp. 264-6, and, of course, Aldous Huxley's *Brave New World.*

9

The Lambeth Resolution

Until August 1958, almost the only argument not yet used for contraception was that it had deep religious and Christian value. The Lambeth Conference of that date has tragically been the means of supplying the missing motivation. It resolved:—

The Conference believes that the responsibility for deciding upon the number and frequency of children has been laid by God upon the consciences of parents everywhere: that this planning, in such ways as are mutually acceptable to husband and wife in Christian conscience, is a right and important factor in Christian family life and should be the result of positive choice before God. Such responsible parenthood, built on obedience to all the duties of marriage, requires a wise stewardship of the resources and abilities of the family as well as a thoughtful consideration of the varying population needs and problems of society and the claims of future generations.[146]

We are told that "the Conference as a whole is responsible only for the formal Resolutions" and not for the Reports of its Special Committees; but to know how to interpret the Resolution, which in itself is ambiguous, we must turn for cues to the Report of the Committee on The Family in Contemporary Society:

> Family planning ought to be the result of thoughtful and prayerful Christian decision. Where it is, Christian husbands and wives need feel no hesitation in offering their decision humbly to God and following it with a clear conscience. The *means* of family planning are in large measure matters of clinical and aesthetic choice, subject to the requirement that they be admissible to the Christian conscience. Scientific studies can rightly help, and do; and Christians have every right to use the gifts of science for proper ends.[147]

The word 'contraceptives cannot, however, be all the time avoided; but when it comes in, the delicacies are respected by the addendum that nothing said about their use in family planning "takes away from the beauty and strength of abstinence mutually accepted." Several other forms of contraception are, however, more or less firmly rejected. Denial of the debitum and *coitus inter-*

ruptus are absolutely excluded. So, also, but less absolutely, is abortion:

> In the strongest terms, Christians reject the practice of induced abortion, or infanticide, which involves the killing of a life already conceived . . . save at the dictate of strict and undeniable medical necessity. The plight of families or, indeed, of governments trapped in hopeless poverty and over-population, may well help us to understand why they think abortion more merciful than the slow starvation which looms ahead. Still, the sacredness of life is, in Christian eyes, an absolute which should not be violated.[148]

Sterilization, too, is tentatively pronounced to be evil, but not quite always or necessarily so:

> All agreed that any government policy of compulsory sterilization as a means of population control is unacceptable to the Christian conscience, at least in our present state of knowledge and understanding; some indeed feel that such a policy could never be justified. Voluntary sterilization, either as a government policy or only as an individual choice, raises many grave questions. It is urged, in some quarters, that sterilization of husband and wife, after the procreation of a proper number of children, seems to be little more than a particularly safe and easy method of family planning . . . Some members felt that in the present state of our

knowledge, we ought not to attempt to judge
finally for the future. The choice of sterilization is a grave one, to be made only in deepest and most conscientious thought, with full
agreement between the spouses . . . Before
any such decision is reached, the most prayerful and serious consideration should be
given, before God, and with the best counsel
from pastor and physician which can be
gained.[149]

The distinguished Anglican theologian, Dr. E.
L. Mascall, criticising the 1958 Lambeth Conference, has written:

The report consists of something like 100,-
000 words; the Conference consisted of 310
bishops and sat for five weeks . . . Quite
inevitably reports of Committees will be
drawn up hastily and will be scanned without their full implications being seen, resolutions will be voted on without their terms
being fully understood, emotional appeals
by enthusiasts will frequently take the place
of thorough and judicious study, fatigue and
inexpertness in debate will lead to uninformed acquiescence . . . Few of the bishops
at Lambeth were trained theologians, and
they met without the assistance of theological assessors to consider matters many of
which were of extreme theological com-
plexity.[150]

Dr. Mascall is concerned only with the Report

on Church Unity and the Church Universal, and
particularly with the questions of the Church of
South India and of Church Union in Ceylon and
North India, and of relations between Anglicans
and Presbyterians. But it is all too easy to see that
the same strictures apply to the Report on the
Family. There is no serious theological study of
the problems in question, no notice whatever taken
of Divine revelation, or of Christian tradition, no
apparent awareness of the religious and moral grav-
ity of what was being decided and approved. Instead of theological plain-speaking we have ambiguity; instead of exact definitions, we have persuasive
re-definitions designed to act as conscience-tran-
quilizers. Perhaps indeed it was the conscience of
the Conference members themselves which first
needed to be tranquilized. A worried conscience is
suggested by the repeated insistence on "thoughtful
and prayerful Christian decision." If Lambeth was
really certain that contraceptives are good, there was
no need to impose on their users all the anxious
heart-searching: what is good is of itself ordained to
God and offered to Him by a Christian's habitual
intention of love of God. But if contraceptives are
evil, no amount of conscientious and prayerful
thought will make them good or their use capable
of being offered to God.

For any serious attempt at reasoning about contraception, we have to turn to the Report of *The
Family in Contemporary Society*,[151] which was prepared by a Group convened at the behest of the

Archbishop of Canterbury in advance of the Lambeth Conference and which prepared Anglican opinion for the Lambeth Resolution. The arguments there advanced for the moral rightness of using contraceptives are reducible to two: (a) The doctrine that contraceptive intercourse is unnatural and therefore inherently sinful is a "metaphysical" doctrine which could not be translated into empirical terms; (b) *Coitus* has "relational and personal" values which justify it even when its "biological values" are deliberately excluded.

We shall illustrate and discuss these theses in turn; first the "anti-metaphysical" argument:

It is by no means easy to sustain the "metaphysical" case on other than a *priori* grounds. It is by no means certain that if human *coitus* has a "given" structure, that structure is disclosed or determined exclusively or even principally by physiological or biological factors . . . Any attempt to define abstractly the empirical factors which guarantee that *coitus* is "natural" must be regarded as misconceived and doomed to failure, for by its very "nature" *coitus* between human beings is not an act of such a kind that it can be so defined . . .[152] It is arguable that it is fully consistent with the nature of human *coitus* as "given," that man, by the responsible exercise of his freedom, should modify certain of its "mechanical" details in order to enrich its relational potentialities.[153]

Some will think that (the "metaphysical") treatment of the question founders on the difficulty of demonstrating that something in the metaphysical realm is bound up with an empirical event of which the essential features can be unalterably specified. In this instance (it may be asked) can we specify exactly those empirical features which are needed to safeguard union? Can we be absolutely sure than any different features necessarily exclude that union? Moreover, no one would maintain that each and every detail of *coitus* is "given" and unalterable.[154]

There is much more talk of a similar kind, about "the philosophical difficulty of conceiving a metaphysical language which is translatable into unmistakable empirical terms"; or against supposing "that a comprehensive deductive metaphysical pattern is also 'given'."[155]

This sort of misunderstanding and misrepresentation of metaphysics belongs to the British philosophy of twenty years ago—to the youth of Professor Ayer. But Ayer himself would scarcely use that language now. This sort of way of defining and "eliminating" metaphysics has been abandoned by intelligent philosophers long ago. In the present context it is anyhow a mere red herring. The question is, whether contraceptive *coitus* is *empirically* the same act as non-contraceptive intercourse, which is agreedly the norm of 'relational' *coitus* between human persons. The answer must be that in

"unmistakable empirical terms" the two are different sorts of acts. All forms of mechanical or chemical contraceptives introduce a separating substance
or a foreign process between the partners in the
exercise of the act itself; and make the act of *coitus*
physically and physiologically, that is, *empirically*
indistinguishable from onanism or *coitus interruptus*
end *effusio extra vas,* which all Anglicans agree to
be immoral.

It is really deplorable to pretend that contraceptive *coitus* is just as natural, normal, relational and
good as non-contraceptive *coitus.* Is it normal to
approach the most loving and personal, tender and
intimate of human relationships with preparations
and instruments appropriate only to a medical examination or a surgical operation? Freud knew better; he wrote:

> Contraceptives available hitherto impair sex-
> ual enjoyment, disturb the finer susceptibili-
> ties of both partners or even act as a direct
> cause of illness.[156]

> It is a characteristic common to all the per-
> versions that in them reproduction as an aim
> is put aside. This is actually the criterion by
> which we judge whether a sexual activity is
> perverse—if it departs from reproduction in
> its aims and pursues the attainment of grati-
> fication independently. You will understand
> therefore that the gulf and turning-point in
> the development of the sexual life lies at the
> point of its subordination to the purposes of

reproduction. Everything that occurs before this conversion takes place, and everything which refuses to conform to it and serves the pursuit of gratification alone, is called by the unhonoured title of "perversion" and as such is despised.[157]

People, alone with their consciences and sincere with themselves and their spouses, know that what they do is a detestable thing. The authors of the Report are evading the moral issue when they tell spouses that the use of contraceptives is a matter of "clinical and aesthetic choice" (how clean and chaste the *words* are for such a sordid act); or even that the "aesthetic" repugnance is of no importance and can be ignored.[158]

The second argument is that contraceptive *coitus* is "relational" and promotive of "the highest personal ends of sexual union."

Likewise it is evident that certain benefits are annexed to *coitus,* but it is impossible to define the precise empirical conditions which must be fulfilled in order to secure such benefits. Again, all that can be said is that the 'relational' blessings conveyed by the act depend upon the quality of the personal relationship of the pair in question who will receive from their intercourse proportionately to what they bring to it.[159]

The fact that man in his freedom stands above nature, and is therefore at liberty to interpret sex in terms of personality and relation and to use it for the achievement of personal and relational ends, leads to the conclusion that contraception is morally right in certain circumstances. Thus man may legitimately extend the range of non-generative *coitus* as it exists in nature, by the use of contraceptive devices, but only so long as this is done in obedience to relational or social needs.[160] There is abundant evidence to show that *coitus* can be both "natural and relationally immoral (as when man and woman exploit one another), and that contraception appears to promote the highest personal ends of sexual union.[161]

We must ask the Anglican experts three questions. The first was put by a "metaphysical" minority in the Group itself: if sexual relations are justified by 'relational' value alone, artificially disconnected from any procreative pattern, how can perverse sexual practices between married people be condemned—if, for them, they have relational value?[162] The second question is the related one: how, on these premises, can heterosexual relations outside of marriage, or adulterous relations, be condemned—if, again, they are claimed to represent deeply-felt personal and relational "needs"? How, finally, on these definitions, can homosexual relations be so defined as to be seen as immoral—if, by the people in question, they are alleged to "promote the highest personal ends of sexual union."[163] How, in other words, do these Anglican experts

hope to evade the conclusions a Russell or a Dr.
Glanville Williams draw from the same contraceptive premises? The only logical moral position for
them to adopt is that espoused by one section in the
Group—the ethics of insight, a form of "situation-
ethics," which, in effect, teaches that *whatever* one
sincerely and prayerfully does is right. And this,
obviously, is only a way of conscientiously deciding
that God has given one a special dispensation from
being moral.[164]

It is sad to see official Anglicanism adhering explicitly to the doctrine that a good intention or end
can make evil actions good.

> In spite of the manifest divergences, there is
> a meeting point of practical importance in
> the judgment that a conscientious decision
> to use contraceptives would in certain cir-
> cumstances be justified.[165] Others would say
> that, although circumstances cannot alter the
> ontological status of *coitus* with contracep-
> tives, they can and do alter its moral status;
> that the modified act, though ontologically
> different from *coitus* during natural infer-
> tility, may on occasion be morally equiva-
> lent, being the best symbol of love and
> union that is eligible in the circumstances.[166]

In such passages, Anglicans seem to make common cause with contemporary analytic philosophers
and the modern tradition in British secular ethics,
in accepting a doctrine of what Miss G. E. M. Anscombe calls 'consequentialism'—the doctrine that

an action ordinarily evil may be morally right "in certain circumstances," where good consequences will follow from it. Miss Anscombe concludes that this doctrine is quite incompatible with Christian ethics, which teaches that there are certain things forbidden "whatever *consequences* threaten."[167] We feel sure, however, that many devout Anglicans have been scandalised and deeply pained by this Report and Resolution; and we can sincerely sympathise with them in the distress of conscience which their Bishops have so regrettably inflicted on them.

The Lambeth Resolution of 1958 has not, of course, been the first Anglican condonation of contraception. The Lambeth Conference of 1930 began it, though more hesitantly, by its Resolution 15:

> Where there is a clearly felt moral obligation to limit or avoid parenthood, the method must be decided on Christian principles. The primary and obvious method is complete abstinence from intercourse . . . in a life of discipline and self-control lived in the the power of the Holy Spirit. Nevertheless in those cases where there is a clearly felt moral obligation to limit or avoid parenthood, and where there is a morally sound reason for avoiding complete abstinence, the Conference agrees that other methods may be used, provided that this is done in the light of the same Christian principles. The Conference records its strong condemnation

of the use of any methods of conception-
control from motives of selfishness, luxury
or mere convenience.[168]

This was the beginning of the tranquillizing of
the Anglican Christian conscience. An American
"motivational research" expert has seen one of the
main jobs of the modern advertiser as "to give
moral permission to have pleasure without guilt."[169]
This is, in final analysis, the effect of the language
of Lambeth. Let us quote Anglicans, lest we be
thought unfair.

Dr. E. L. Mascall has written about Lambeth,
1958 (he is speaking, as we noted, of the Report on
Reunion, but what he says is, in our view, even
more applicable to the Report on the Family):

We should do all in our power to resist the
debasement of theological thought and language that has progressively taken place
. . . This has occurred in two ways. One is
by the painstaking construction of statements, formulas and rites that are deliberately meant to be ambiguous . . . The other
is by the substitution of vague terms of non-
theological provenance for the precise terms
of traditional theology . . . What is at stake
is . . . nothing less than the function of
human speech as the medium for the communication of truth . . . We can easily over-
look the fact that 'doublethink' has seriously
invaded the realm of Christian life . . . I do
not see how any man can engage for very

long in the task of devising ambiguous forms of words without blunting his sense of the awful claims of truth.[170]

The Bishop of Bradford, Right Rev. Dr. Blunt, said of Lambeth, 1930:

I should have thought it was quite obvious that in the case of a resolution, the true meaning of which depended entirely upon qualifications, vested interests would use the resolution for their own purposes with all the qualifications left out, and this is exactly what has happened. It has been to the interest of those trading in contraceptive appliances to represent themselves as having the support of the Lambeth Conference and they have done it.[171]

They are doing it again. The following advertisement has been appearing in *The Chemist and Druggist* since Lambeth, 1958:

The Anglican Bishops endorse family planning.

"Family planning, in such ways as are mutually acceptable to husband and wife in Christian conscience . . . is a right and important factor in Christian family life."— Report of the Ninth Lambeth Conference. Commenting on the report, the Archbishop of Canterbury said: ". . . there is clearly a divine obligation to plan your family and not have them by accident." Asked if he personally advocated family planning, the

Archbishop replied: "What the conference says is that it is a necessity and I agree." With these words, the 310 Anglican Bishops have given their blessing to the principles of family planning. In setting forth this enlightened point of view, they have removed the confusion and controversy which have surrounded the subject for years. Their wise and human approach will be endorsed by thoughtful people everywhere . . . Write for the discreet "Family Planning Requisites" shelf strip, which shows that you are an XXX stockist. It will bring you extra business—so put it on display.[172]

Let us leave the last word on this subject to Chesterton. He wrote after Lambeth, 1930,[173] an article called "The Surrender upon Sex." He said that his parents, not very orthodox Christians, would have regarded birth-prevention exactly as they would have regarded infanticide. He said that he would certainly have left Anglicanism after Lambeth, 1930, if he had not already left it. He concluded:

My concern is . . . with all to whom I might once have looked to defend the country of the Christian altars. They ought surely to know that the foe now on the frontiers offers no terms of compromise; but threatens a complete destruction. And they have sold the pass.[174]

[146] *The Lambeth Conference, 1958. The Encyclical Letter, etc.* S.P.C.K. 1958, 1. 57, No. 115.

[147] Op. cit., 2, 147. Compare *The Family in Contemporary Society,* S.P.C.K., London, 1958, pp. 13, 16, 143, on "the extension of the responsible use of science into the realm of procreation."

[148] Op. cit., 2, 148.

[149] Op. cit., 2, 148-9.

[150] *Lambeth 1958 and Christian Unity,* The Faith Press, London, p. 6. One's curiosity is aroused by the fact that a press report on the eve of the Conference (see the *Observer,* 13th July, 1958) announced that the Committee on the Family would have as vice-chairman Dr. R. C. Mortimer, Bishop of Exeter, "the most learned moral theologian at Lambeth, and one who takes a rigorist canon law view on questions of marriage and parenthood." (Dr. Cecil Northcott). Dr. Mortimer, formerly Regius Professor of Moral and Pastoral Theology in the University of Oxford, was, however, not even a member of the Committee which actually drew up the Report. Judging from his sound theological positions in the Report of the Archbishop of Canterbury's Commission on Artificial Human Insemination, of which he was a leading member, Dr. Mortimer would not have been either uninformed or acquiescent in the matter of this unfortunate Lambeth Report on the Family.

[151] S.P.C.K., London, 1958.

[152] It would be hard to find a more beautiful example of *petitio principii.*

[153] Op. cit., p. 146.

[154] Op. cit., p. 129. Compare p. 147: "It is pertinent, therefore, to ask whether "natural" coitus (in the traditional moral-theological sense) is not simply an arbitrary *a priori* concept to which there is no correspondence in reality." Compare p. 15. "(The 'anti-metaphysical' view) cannot be overthrown unless we are prepared to maintain that the nature of coition is 'given' in every particular and for ever, in all its physical and metaphysical aspects, and so placed outside the realm of human decision."

[155] Op. cit., p. 130. In the recent B.B.C. series of talks on "Christian doctrine and divorce," Canon Carpenter condemned the notion of marriage as absolutely indissoluble by

calling it a "metaphysical abstraction . . . without empirical content and independent of (the) life-history of marriage." (The Anglican Canon Bentley had effectively disposed of such sophistry in the preceding talk.) See *The Listener*, 14th and 21st August, 1958.

[156] "Sexual Morality and Nervousness" (1908), in *Collected Papers*, v II, Hogarth Press, London, 1933.

[157] *Introductory Lectures on Psycho-analysis*, E. tr. by Joan Rivière, 2nd edit., Allen and Unwin, London, 1952, p. 266; cfr. Freud's *Collected Papers*, Vol. I, International Psycho-analytical Press, London, 1924, pp. 88, 238. Compare Mihanovitch, Schnepp and Thomas, *Marriage and the Family*, pp. 105-6; S. de Lestapis, *La limitation des naissances*, pp. 92 ff.; Keenan and Ryan, *Marriage: A Medical and Sacramental Study*, Sheed & Ward, London, 1955, pp. 119-124; Guchteneere, op. cit., pp. 115-173; Leo J. Latz, *The Rhythm*, Chicago, 1953, pp. 54, 129-131; Ch. Mertens de Wilmars, *Psycho-pathologie de l'Anti-conception*, Centre d'Etudes Laennec, Lethielleux, Paris, 1955, pp. 52 ff., 79 ff., 102, and passim. It is significant that statistics of suicide show twice as many suicides among childless married women as among unmarried women: see G. Deshaies, *Psychologie du Suicide*, P.U.F., Paris, 1947, pp. 31-2 and foll.

[158] The passage we refer to reads: "(The so-called aesthetic objection) as a rule . . . rests upon a mental image of a particular technique. In any case it is in the highest degree subjective. In the matter of the *usus matrimonii* no reliance can be placed on the emotional reactions of individuals, since such reactions are so much governed by a person's sexual experience—or lack of it."—Op. cit., p. 133. The "moral absolution" use of language is frequently noticed nowadays. Nazi concentration camp jailers used the words 'clean,' 'practical,' 'pure,' of the hygienic aspects of their horrible work: "they thought in chemical and statistical terms in order not to be aware of their deeper moral guilt." See Joost A. Meerloo, *Mental Seduction and Menticide*, Cape, London, 1957, p. 213.

[159] Op. cit., p. 146.

[160] Op. cit., p. 145.

[161] Op. cit., p. 147.

[162] Op. cit., p. 135. "Once subission to the 'given' pattern is

abandoned," this minority rightly say, "all kinds of varia-
tions on the sexual theme which heighten satisfaction can
appear to be enrichments of the sexual life." They see that
contraception could mean that "man may, without knowing
or intending it, be stepping over the boundary between the
world of Christian marriage and what one may call the
world of Aphrodite—the world of sterile eroticism." Compare p. 130. The Anglican surrender on contraception contrasts with the more Christian official stand on divorce. The
Archbishop of Canterbury has written: "If the Church were
to marry divorced persons there would be no way left in
which it could bear effective witness before the world to the
standard of Christ . . . If the Church were to make exceptions it would raise a number of unanswerable questions."
Dr. G. F. Fisher, *Problems of Marriage and Divorce,*
S.P.C.K., London 1955, p. 21.

163 Compare M. J. Buckley, *Morality and the Homosexual,*
Sands, London, 1959, XV; S. de Lestapis, *La limitation des
naissances,* pp. 97-8. It is significant that when Anglican
Commissions and Study Groups reported, as they have done
in recent years, on the immortality of homosexuality and
of artificial insemination, they did so on the basis of a
theology of sex and marriage derived from Catholic tradition
and close to Catholic teaching. See e.g. *Artificial Human Insemination,* S.P.C.K., London, 1948, pp. 43-54. Note particularly p. 45: "(The ends of marriage) are, of course,
three: procreation, union and the 'society, help and comfort'
which a man 'ought to have' from his wife, and she from
him . . . Nevertheless (the second two ends) . . . are not
merely secondary and subsidiary to the first; they are nor-
mally included within and powerfully assist it. The refusal
of parenthood impairs the union as certainly as the with-
holding of 'help and comfort' denies it. All three ends are
closely related and are mutually dependent. The attempt to
pursue only one, or two, of them by deliberate exclusion of
the third is to seek a relationship not properly that of marriage. That so many persons in our society make this attempt
(albeit unconsciously) does not invalidate the Christian
doctrine of marriage, although it goes far to explain the
contemporary sexual disorder." This is obviously, for the
Lambeth majority, the "rigorist canon law view," associated

with Dr. R. C. Mortimer, who was expected to be, but was not, a member of the Lambeth Committee on the Family.

164 See op. cit., pp. 130-1: "Eschewing any kind of *a priori* starting point, except the broadest background of Christian doctrine, it begins by postulating a case in which man and wife have conscientiously decided that in their particular circumstances the use of contraceptives can be made a part of the offering of their marriage to the glory of God. Here is a claim to valid insight . . . Those who adopt (this view) do not claim to enunciate incontrovertible Christian principles of universal validity which could stand as axioms for the development of a deductive ethic. (Oxford moral philosophy again!) The appeal to insight is, in their opinion, fundamental . . ."

165 Op. cit., p. 14.

166 Op. cit., p. 137. Compare the Reservation by Very Rev. Canon A. A. Luce, Fellow of T.C.D., formerly Professor of Moral Philosophy in the University of Dublin, to the *Reports* of the Irish *Commission on Emigration and other Population Problems,* Stationery Office, Dublin, 1954, pp. 230-1: "I dissociate myself from the unqualified and unargued condemnation of contraceptives. I do not advocate their use. I know little about them. But I am a trained student of moral problems . . . Public morals must be protected by law, where necessary, and I can see that safeguards of law are necessary in this matter. But the essence of the moral problem must be distinguished from accidental features, and at all costs the right of private judgment in private matters must be preserved. Is it consonant with morality to limit the size of one's family by the avoidance of conception? It is. That prior and major question has been decided in the affirmative by reason, by common sense and by general consent. In the light of that decision, and in the light of the circumstances of modern life and modern homes, the relatively minor questions as to the means employed should be approached." Canon Luce, as his friends know, is a kind and courteous and lovable gentleman, in the best sense of this sometimes misused term. But how can he fail to see that he has written here a shocking statement? If it meant what it says, it would seem to condone *coitus interruptus* and sterilization; and to leave no reason for absolute condemnation

of abortion as a means of population control. It is, on the face of it, an acceptance of the doctrine that the end justifies the means.

167 See the Journal *Philosophy,* XXXII, January, 1958, p. 10. Compare Miss Anscombe's famous broadcast: "Does Oxford Moral Philosophy corrupt Youth?"; see *The Listener,* 14th February, 1957.

168 See Halliday Sutherland, *Control of Life,* Burns Oates, London, 1944, p. 104. Resolution 16 reads: "The Conference further records its abhorrence of the sinful practice of abortion."

169 See Vance Packard, *The Hidden Persuaders,* pp. 57, 263.

170 Op. cit., p. 18.

171 Halliday Sutherland, op. cit., p. 106.

172 The advertisers are, of course, not *solely* interested in the principles of "Christian family life"! They make profits too: huge ones. One estimate says 1,100 per cent. on cost of manufacture, 90 per cent for wholesalers; see Halliday Sutherland, op. cit., pp. 59-60. Dr. Fisher has since reiterated his view, that "family planning" is not merely right but is "a positive Christian duty." Writing in his diocesan bulletin, he says: "For some time past it has been seen to be an evident Christian duty in England as elsewhere that parents should be wise and control the planning of a family in order to avoid as far as possible putting an unfair physical burden on the mother or any unfair handicap upon the children or any unreasonable liability upon society." He protests against "Roman Catholic pronouncements" for causing "misunderstanding as to the general Christian attitude to it." See the daily press, 24th March, 1960.

173 It was in the same year, 1930, that Pope Pius XI, in *Casti Connubii,* gravely pronounced: "Wherefore, since there are some who, openly departing from the Christian teaching which has been handed down uninterruptedly from the beginning, have in recent times thought fit solemnly to preach another doctrine concerning this practice, the Catholic Church . . . standing erect amidst this moral devastation, raises her voice in sign of her divine mission to keep the chastity of the marriage contract unsullied by this ugly stain, and through Our mouth proclaims anew; that any use of matrimony whatsoever, in the exercise of which the act is

deprived, by human interference, of its natural power to procreate life, is an offence against the law of God and of nature, and that those who commit it are guilty of a grave sin."
[174] *The Well and the Shallows,* Sheed & Ward, London,
1937, pp. 37-44. One can sympathise with Mrs. Wooton who
writes: ". . . in ethics . . . we have the spectacle of doctrine
which claims divine authority being steadily withdrawn from
the particular to the general . . . Each of these retreats, however, involving as it does the surrender of a previously final
position, threatens the fundamental security of religious
morals and provokes the unbeliever to ask 'Why stop
here?' " (*Testament for Social Science,* Allen & Unwin, London, 1950, pp. 132-3.)

10

Abortion

Dr. Glanville Williams spreads himself over two long chapters on the question of abortion, chapters in which theology, morality, law, medicine, sociology and statistics are thoroughly mixed. The general premises of his argument will be already familiar; we need not trouble to pursue all the varied details of their application. We shall examine only his treatment of the religious and moral issue; then look at his case for 'liberalisation' of the law on abortion in the light of the "social facts" and the present state of medical science and medical opinion.

On the moral issue Dr. Glanville Williams's major argument is that the fetus is not a human person and that therefore its life is not an absolute value.

> Is the sanctity of the embryo or fetus a moral absolute, or are we to be allowed to look to utilitarian consideration? . . . On the moral plane, no utilitarian argument has any effect upon the opinion that the unborn child is as much entitled to protection as the

adult. To a large extent it defies rational enquiry and solution, since it pertains to metaphysics or emotion, and not to empirical
facts. The view that human personality mys-
tically begins with the ovum cannot be refuted any more than it can be proved.[175]

Perhaps the soul is a miraculous addition to
the act of fertilisation . . . something coming
from and returning along a divine dimension
which is outside the ken of a biologist . . .
Can it be said, with any degree of reality,
that the week- or month-old embryo is an
existing human being?[176]

It is to be hoped, we may say in passing, that
Anglican theologians will take note of where the
"anti-metaphysics" road, on which they are travel-
ling, leads. It was a mistake for Dr. Glanville Williams to bring biology into his argument; for then
we can ask biologists to check his statements. They
assure us that human personality, as biological science understands it, does begin with and is verified
in the fertilized ovum. All the gene-determined
characters of the adult human personality are already present in germ in the ovum. There is no
break in the continuous development of the human
organism from conception until death; no point at
which any vital principle could "supervene" which
was not there at the moment of fertilization. The
soul enters the scene when sperm and ovum meet;
it moves thenceforth along a biological as well as a
divine dimension. The question which Dr. Glanville

Williams so heavily labours, of the time of animation of the fetus, has been settled by biology.

Let us listen to a Doctor, making his own the words of a Professor of Medicine of the University of Strasbourg:

> From the moment of fertilisation of the ovum there is, in the silence of the fetal site, a prodigious hive of vital activity . . . all the physico-chemical processes occurring there have a meaning . . .; there is a vital principle co-ordinating and directing all these mechanisms. A soul is there. It is there from the instant of fertilisation. Fertilisation occurs precisely because the meeting of the paternal and maternal life-cells is the occasion for the infusion of a soul into a new child-cell . . . There is no break, no interruption, between the stage at which the soul displays biological vitality, the stage at which its cognitive powers appear, and the stage when all can see the riches of its power of personal reflection. There is no way of marking a moment when the soul passes from mere vegetable life to animal life and then to mental life. But this is precisely because, from the very first moment of life, a human soul is present and acting.[177]

Here is the empirical fact on which our "metaphysical" morality is built; a fertilized ovum is a living human being; to kill it is murder; and one may never murder for any reason whatever. It is not a question, as Dr. Glanville Williams and so many others think, of "which life" is the more valuable, but of whether one may murder one human being to save another. Dr. Glanville Williams has much to say in this context about the Double Effect Doctrine.[178] It would be tedious to track down his mistakes; it is anyhow unnecessary. The "double effect" principle says fundamentally one thing and a simple thing, but a bed-rock thing: it says that, if something is morally evil in itself, it can never be right to do it in any circumstances or for any good results whatever. Good intentions or good consequences do not make evil good or wrong right. This is what Dr. Glanville Williams impatiently calls the "dogma" that evil cannot be done that good may come."[179] This differentiates Catholic moral teaching from all scientific humanist, relativist, or 'situation' ethics. It is the important issue in all contemporary moral discussion. It is perhaps the only ultimately important issue in all moral discussion at any time.

It is impossible to construct a definition of ovum or embryo or fetus which will allow destruction of them and forbid destruction of adult human beings. It is impossible so to define feticide that it can be pronounced morally right and murder can still be called morally wrong. A Catholic writer on Medical Ethics has said:

> It would, indeed, be interesting to hear a proponent of therapeutic abortion define murder. If such a person defines "murder"

accurately he will not be able to justify therapeutic abortion. If some unique definition
of murder is given, the path is opened immediately for the wholesale destruction of
human life whenever notable temporal good
would thereby be achieved.[180]

The Reverend Mr. Fletcher and Dr. Glanville
Williams provide proof conclusive of the truth of
this proposition. The former suggests definitions
which make the differentia between fetus and human being, or between the "pre-personal" and the
"personal," consist in consciousness:

> (The sound course to take is . . .) to deny
> that the right to life claimed for a fetus is
> valid, because a fetus is not a moral or
> personal being, since it lacks freedom, self-
> determination, rationality, the ability to chose
> either means or ends, and knowledge of its
> circumstances.[181]

On this definition we must equally deny the
right to life claimed for infants, imbeciles, mental
defectives, psychotics and many neurotics, dotards,
sick persons who are unconscious.[182] The Reverend
Mr. Fletcher, however, feels anyhow that mental
defectives should never have been allowed to be
born.[183] He advocates usefulness to the community
and 'power of service' as criteria of the value of
living.[184] And one of his clinching arguments for
euthanasia is that if or since abortion is morally
lawful, euthanasia must be so too.

. . . There are common exceptions to the

rule against medical homicide. If one can be made at the beginning of life (abortion) why not also at the end of life (euthanasia)? The one situation is no more absolute than the order. There is no more stigma in the one than in the other. On personalistic grounds we could say that there is less question morally in euthanasia, for in euthanasia a merciful death is chosen in co-operation with a person whose integrity is threatened by disintegration, whereas an embryo in therapeutic abortion has no personal value or development at stake and cannot exercise the moral qualities of freedom and knowledge.[185]

We have already seen that Dr. Glanville Williams's philosophy of life does not exclude infanticide in the name of human progress.

A serious increase in the number of degenerate children might well force mankind to a policy of 'weeding out' which is at variance with our present humanitarian outlook.[286]

He is fond of the argument: "the next logical step would be . . ."; "there is no logical stopping place . . ." [187]

We can now appreciate more fully the words of the late Pope Pius XII:

The life of an innocent person is untouchable and every direct attack or agression against it violates one of the fundamental laws without which secure living in human society is impossible.[188]

The inviolability of the life of an innocent person does not depend upon its greater or lesser value. Anyone who will weigh the awful consequences which would follow from allowing the inviolability of an innocent life to depend upon its "value," will have no difficulty in accepting the reasons for the Church's teaching.[189]

Dr. Glanville Williams say: "If we protect the fetus by law, it should be for reasons relating to the well-being of existing human beings."[190] This is exactly what the Pope said: except that the Pope said *right to life* instead of *well-being* of existing human beings. And the right to life of all human beings, just *qua* human, is the presupposition and precondition of anyone's right to life or of anyone's well-being.

Dr. Glanville Williams does speak occasionally as a lawyer. When he does, it is always for 'bold,' 'progressive' and 'imaginative' legislation. In the present context he wants a much more liberal interpretation of the term 'therapeutic' abortion, so as to allow abortion not merely on eugenic but on very wide 'psychiatric,' 'compassionate' and 'socio-medical' grounds. He sees the Macnaghten judgment in Rex *v.* Bourne as enshrining the doctrine that

the interest of the mother in living a single extra day is preferred to the life of the child . . .[191]

Looking at the question on principle, there seems no good reason why the defence should not be extended to cases where pregnancy is terminated for the purpose of preventing serious physical injury to the mother (e.g. impairment of sight or hearing) . . . The mother's life must be considered in relation to its quality as well as to its duration. Serious physical injury to the mother, who is a human being with the full human capacity for pain, is an evil greater both morally and socially than the destruction of the fetus, at any rate if the fetus is in an early stage of development . . . Alternatively the opinion may well be held that the life of the mother should be preferred to the life of the fetus at all stages.[192]

'Psychiatric,' 'social' and 'socio-medical' indications are such vague terms that they offer a rich harvest to abortion-specialists and their legal advisers. 'Therapeutic' can, by a policy of calculated gradualness, be stretched to cover "the belief that childbirth would be injurious to the mother," or that rearing the child after birth would "impose a strain" on the mother's health; it can include "emotional stress" in the mother, due, perhaps, to fear that her child may be defective . . . (or have a cleft palate) . . .; "a supporting therapeutic reason" could be that "it will be bad for the mother's health to bring up an ailing infant." [193] And if the mother does not have "emotional stress," she can always be given some:

> The legal course is apparently for the doctor to tell the mother of the risk in order to bring on the worry and then to abort on account of the worry. This plan doubtless works well enough unless the mother happens to be feeble-minded, in which case her child must be allowed to be born.[194]

If this is meant by Dr. Glanville Williams as a joke, many will feel that the joke, in this context, is in doubtful taste.

All we need say about this is that it is utterly out of touch with the present state of medical science, and that the proposals of our 'progressive' lawyer would in fact put back the clock of medicine by at least twenty-five years. It is an interesting exercise to look over text-books of midwifery in this century and note the number and type of "indications for termination of pregnancy." Nothing is so conspicuous as the fact that, as revised edition succeeds edition, the "indications" become fewer, more qualified, more doubtful, more hesitant, more ashamed. The progress of midwifery is in direct proportion to respect for the inviolability of the fetus; it is in inverse proportion to the tolerance of therapeutic abortion. A great French obstetrician has said that his colleagues, whether Christian or not, whether religious or atheist, have in common "a fundamental moral principle, clearly Christian in its essence, which expresses itself in the profound respect they have for the human ovum."[195]

Let us ask medical experts, who know something about the subject, to speak for themselves. G. F. Gibberd writes:

> When the question of terminating a pregnancy is being considered, it is important to remember that the induction of abortion is an operation involving risks which exceed those of child-birth. Termination of pregnancy in the early months is not therefore to be preferred to labour at term . . . if, because of complicating circumstances, labour involves a risk to the mother, it is almost certain that induction of abortion will, in the same circumstances, involve risk at least as great.[196]

R. W. Johnstone and R. J. Kellar are equally definite:

> In modern obstetrics increasing importance is being paid to the preservation of fetal life and we try to avoid (a) the premature interruption of pregnancy, and (b) methods of interference (with pregnancy) likely to prejudice the child's chances of survival . . . The success of this modern outlook is based upon increased facilities for blood transfusion and on improved technique in Caesarean section.[197]

Docteur L. Portes, Clinical Professor of Gynaecology and Obstetrics in the Faculty of Medicine of

Paris, Member of the French Academy of Medicine and sometime president of the National Council of the Ordre des Médecins, writes:

> From all that we have said, it follows that, in the final analysis, there are, in practice, in present-day conditions, no really absolute indications of therapeutic abortion . . . If we could say one day—as Pinard did about embryotomy on the living child—"therapeutic abortion is a thing of the past," we would have eliminated from the exercise of our art the last performance to survive from the days of barbarism . . . We are, in any case, certainly obliged to declare that the rigorous dogmatic attitude which has been adopted all down the centuries, in this regard, by the Roman Catholic Church, is in no manner opposed by our medical knowledge; but that, on the contrary, the very evolution of our art enables us to foresee a time, perhaps not too far distant, when therapeutic abortion will have shared the fate of embryotomy on the living infant.[198]

Let us leave the final word to another Ulster Protestant gynaecologist, Mr. Harold Ian M'Clure, Clinical Lecturer in Midwifery and Gynaecology in the Queen's University of Belfast. Giving the opening address of the Winter Session in October, 1954, Mr. M'Clure said:

> The Christian Church (or at least important sections of it) has expressed its views on such

matters as euthanasia and the mother-child
problem. With regard to the former, there is
no fundamental difference of opinion between the Church and the medical profession. With regard to the latter, the equality
of mother and fetus is an authoritative
dogma of the Roman Catholic Church.
"The life of each is equally sacred," said
Pope Pius XI in his encyclical *Casti Connubii,* "and no one has the power, not even
the public authority, to destroy it." There
has, however, been an important advance
in medical skill which makes the problem
a much more remote one than it once was.
The sulfa drugs and anti-biotics together
have made delivery by Caesarean section so
much safer, even in the infected cases (e.g.
a failed forceps delivery), that the operation
of craniotomy on the living child is now no
longer practised; and it is probably true to
say that better ante-natal care and prognosis
may do much to eliminate the partial disaster of the failed forceps delivery. Another
advance is in the care of the premature infant, so that babies have been reared even
in the sixth month. The old seventh month
need no longer be a limit of viability for the
obstetrician. The problem of morbidity in
the early weeks of pregnancy was often
solved in the past by terminating the pregnancy. With pernicious vomiting now reced-

ing into an ugly past, the modern indications are mostly the toxemias of pregnancy and it is doubtful if there is, in fact, any indication for termination of pregnancy before the viability of the child. Moreover, it is admitted by all authorities that the risk of operating is often greater than the danger of an expectant line of treatment. I mention these matters to show that, even when medical practice has not fully approximated to the teaching of the Roman Catholic Church, the advance of medical science is bringing the ideal of both bodies (the preservation of the life of both mother and child), much nearer than it once was.[199]

Clearly medicine does not share Dr. Glanville Williams's view of which direction is forward. But he has an ambivalent attitude towards medical and social facts. He is always accusing Catholic moralists of denying the relevance of empirical enquiry, of ignoring the evidence of the social facts and of the social effects of morality. Arguing for increased facilities for legal abortion, he urges that this will control the plague of illegal abortions. Not many pages after, however, surveying the experience of legalized abortion in Sweden and Denmark, he unperturbedly writes:

Another factual ground of criticism (about the Swedish legislation) . . . is that it has not substantially reduced the number of illegal abortions; according to one opinion, these have actually become more numerous because the legislation has helped to remove the feeling that abortion is wrong, and indeed promotes an abortion mentality which extends to all women who have become unintentionally pregnant . . . Some such result is to be expected, because it cannot be hoped that legislation which restricts the grounds (!) for legal abortion will entirely displace the illegal operator . . . Although the social result is rather to add the total of legal abortions to the total of illegal abortions than to reduce the number of illegal abortions, a body of medical opinion refuses to regret the legal abortions on this account.[200]

A Danish doctor is quoted:

Perhaps the law has thus indirectly resulted in more cases of illegal abortions than it has directly prevented, but on the whole most of the physicians in Denmark would certainly not like to do without this liberlised legislation.[201]

Evidently, for the scientific humanists, legalized abortion is just intuitively seen as inherently good, quite apart from its consequences;—and the social facts have nothing to do with their case. There is something sublime about a faith so superior to mere proof or logic or evidence or fact.

[175] Pp. 204-5.
[176] P. 208.

[177] Dr. René Biot, quoting Professor Max Aron, in *Santé Humaine*, Plon, Paris, 1949, p. 80. A doctor thus describes his first sight, as a student, of an induced abortion: "To see what had been a live, pulsating and intriguing structure turned into an inert mass in the space of minutes, left one with an overwhelming sense of fear . . . It convinced one that destruction of life could never be part of a doctor's role; it was against the very essence of what his mission is." —Keenan and Ryan, *Marriage, A Medical and Sacramental Study*, p. 147. It is incredible that a biologist like Sir Julian Huxley should, in a recent B.B.C. Television brains-trust, have said that the use of abortifacient drugs in the early stages of pregnancy cannot properly be called abortion for there is nothing expelled but a mass of blood-clot. This is, biologically, nonsense. The Rev. Mr. Fletcher writes: "The embryo before birth is a portion of the mother, which may be excised if it threatens her life." op. cit., p. 152. This is both biologically and psychologically untrue. A mother has written: "No one who has ever lost a baby, however early in pregnancy, can doubt that the overwhelming sorrow and disappointment—often far more vehement than the mother herself had expected—is testimony to the fact that it was indeed a human being which died." See Lady Pakenham, in *Catholic Approaches*, London, 1955, pp. 116-7.

[178] Pp. 183-7; 285-6.

[179] P. 184.

[180] Charles J. McFadden, *Medical Ethics*, F. A. Davis Co., Philadelphia, Third Edition, 1953, p. 166.

[181] P. 152.

[182] In fact, anyone who is unconscious, e.g. who has suffered a stroke or is in a coma. Dismissing brusquely objections against euthanasia-by-patients'-consent, the Reverend Mr. Fletcher says: "These seem unreal problems, purely logical in character, if it is held, as we do hold, that a patient who has completely lost the power to communicate has passed into a submoral state, outside the forum of consciousness and beyond moral being. Being no longer responsive he is no longer responsible. Conscience and consciousness are inseparable . . . Without (consciousness) personality is gone and there is no longer a 'person' . . ." (p. 201, compare pp. 168, 191).

[183] P. 164. "It is a grave wrong and a betrayal of the Christian concept of personality . . . to allow stunted and defective lives to be propagated when the means are available in medicine to prevent it. It would seem blasphemous to assert that God wills or purposes that defective children should be born. Let the theologians, in their speculative systems based on first causes, solve in some other way the problem of conflict between God's goodness and the fact of evil in the chromosomes."

[184] P. 202.

[185] P. 205.

[186] P. 35; cf. pp. 31 ff., and 293, cited in chapter One.

[187] He says, about the law on abortion: "The logical next step would be to take the medical profession out of the Act" (p. 146). Compare p. 215: "Once abortion is permitted to preserve the mother's health and working capacity, there can be no convincing reason for stopping short at this point and refusing to take account of wider social grounds."

[188] Address to the Italian Catholic Association of Midwives, 29th October, 1951; see *Catholic Documents,* VI, Salesian Press, London, 1952, p. 3.

[189] Address to the Family Associations of Italy, 26th October, 1951; see R. Kothen, *Directives Récentes de l'Église de Concernant l'Exercise de la Médecine,* Louvain, 1952, p. 93.

[190] P. 208. He says (p. 205): "The major premise, the general value-judgment "Killing human beings is wrong" is not in question." It quite precisely is.

[191] P. 152.

[192] Pp. 153-4. Dr. Glanville Williams says laws against abortion have all been made by males, and feminine opinion is all for repeal of them (p. 203). Simone de Beauvoir holds the exact opposite: and she should know *le deuxième sexe*— and is not a Christian; see Ch. Mertens de Wilmars, *Psychopathologie de l'anticonception,* pp. 77-8; compare the quotations in the same sense from Forel, Schokaert, Duyckaerts and other psychologists on pp. 75-92. Dr. Glanville Williams himself notes that abortion "even when performed for therapeutic reasons, is felt by some to be unclean or in some way discreditable" (p. 213); and he refers to, but makes light of, Scandinavian evidence of the "self-reproaches" and other

"mental troubles" caused to some women by the perform-
ance of legal abortion. (See pp. 220-1).

[193]Pp. 155-163.

[194] P. 163.

[195] Dr. L. Portes, *L'Avortement* (see infra), p. 7. This is,
of course, the "fundamental moral principle" of European
medical tradition from the Hippocratic Oath (". . . I shall
never supply any woman with an abortive pessary . . .") to
the Geneva Medical Oath, approved by the World Health
Organization in 1948 (". . . I shall keep absolute respect for
human life, from the time of conception . . .").

[196] *A Short Textbook of Midwifery,* Fifth Edition, 1953,
J. & A. Churchill, p. 476. Compare pp. 213, 218, 251, 255
et saepe. On "neurological indications" Gibberd drily remarks: "Most neurologists are agreed that pregnancy has a
bad effect on the progress of chronic degenerative processes
of the central nervous system . . . It must be remembered,
however, that these diseases tend to progress quite apart
from pregnancy, so that it is sometimes difficult to know the
measure of responsibility to attribute to pregnancy when a
patient is left permanently worse after delivery . . . In deciding whether or not to advise termination of pregnancy in
these cases, there will sometimes be a difference of opinion
between the neurologist and the obstetrician" (pp. 267-8).
Compare L. Williams, *Aids to Obstetrics,* Twelfth Edition,
1953, Baillière, Tindall & Cox, London, p. 241: "Practi-
tioners should beware of the psychopathic individual who
threatens suicide or stages a dramtic attempt with a view to
blackmailing the practitioner into terminating an unwanted
pregnancy."

[197] *A Textbook of Midwifery,* Fifteenth Edition, 1952, A. &
C. Black, London, p. 401; cf. pp. 261, 276-7 et saepe.

[198] In *L'Avortement,* Centre d'Études Laennec, Lethielleux,
Paris, pp. 16-18.

[199] *The Ulster Medical Journal,* November, 1954, p. 97.

[200] P. 219. He called the Swedish experience "depressing" in
broadcast discussions on the B.B.C. on 22nd January, 1959,
and on 11th February, 1959. The number of legal abortions
in Sweden rose from 703 in 1943 to 6,328 in 1951. In 1950
there were 51 abortions for each 1,000 parturients. Compare
S. de Lestapis, *La limitation des naissances,* pp. 60-6.

[201] P. 223. Since the legalizing legislation of 1939, legal abortions have increased from 500 to 5,000 yearly. There are probably, in addition, a steady 12,000 illegal abortions yearly, in a population of some four millions (p. 222).

11

Sterilization

Dr. Glanville Williams began his lecture on sterilization by making it clear that "it is not a desexing operation."[202] This is a good beginning for an investigation of his ideas on the subject; for the purpose of sterilization, in his mind, is to permit people who do not wish, or who "ought not to be allowed" to have children, to have unrestricted sexual indulgence "without complications." Given the limited efficacy of contraception and the expense of abortion, sterilization is the logical conclusion of the new sexual ethic.[203] Much wider use of it will be required before the world is made safe for "free love." Meanwhile, "irrational arguments," "restrictive policies," old-fashioned views" stand in the way of legal impunity for "sterilization of convenience,"[204] and there is admitted to be a "philosophical problem" involved in compulsory sterilization.[205]

Until these "moral road-blocks"—to use a phrase from the Reverend Mr. Fletcher—are removed, there is more hope for a legal break-through in the direction of legalized "eugenic sterilization"; and Dr. Glanville Williams feels that this is at least

better than doing nothing, and will do for a start.[206]
Two British Committees have considered this question. The first was appointed by the Council of the
British Medical Association in 1930 to investigate
problems of mental deficiency and it reported in
1932. Dr. Glanville Williams does not refer to it.
Clearly, from his point of view, it was "old-fashioned" and "unimagative." It concluded:

> It is not practicable to suggest the steriliza-
> tion of Mendelian Carriers as a class. For a
> *small* number of mental defectives . . . ster-
> ilization might be advisable, if (*a*) restricted
> to suitable cases, (*b*) not utilized to per-
> mit discharge of those who need institutional
> care, (*c*) adequate supervision is exercised
> to prevent promiscuous sexual intercourse
> . . . Even widely applied to mental defec-
> tives, sterilization would cause no apprecia-
> ble difference in the number of such in the
> community for many generations.[207]

The Second Committee (a "strong committee,"[208] this one!) was a Departmental Committee
of the Ministry of Health, known as the Brock
Committee. Set up in 1932, it reported to Parlia-
ment, through the Minister of Health, in 1933. This
Committee was

> impressed by the dead weight of social in-
> efficiency and individual misery which is
> entailed by the existence in our midst of
> over a quarter of a million mental defectives

and a far larger number of persons who . . .
are mentally subnormal.

It recommended that voluntary sterilization should
be legalized, under safeguard,

> not only for mental defectives and persons
> who have suffered from mental disorder, but
> for persons who suffer from or are believed
> to be carriers of grave physical disabilities
> that have been shown to be transmissible,
> and also persons believed to be likely to
> transmit mental disorder or defect.[209]

The date of this Report is historic: 1933 was
the year of the notorious Nazi compulsory sterilization laws.[210] This was worse than a "philosophical
problem" for sterilizationists. As Dr. Glanville Williams puts it:

> The cause of eugenics suffered a set-back
> through its unwelcome (!) espousal by the
> Nazi government in Germany in the law of
> 1933 . . . The authoritarian character of the
> measure, and the suspicion that it was used
> as a racial and political instrument rather
> than as a scientific one—suspicions intensi-
> fied by the way in which this legislation was
> followed closely by mass-killing on racial
> grounds—brought the whole case of eugen-
> ics into a disrepute among freedom-loving
> peoples that is only slowly being dissi-
> pated.[211]

However, freedom-loving peoples soon forget.
Hitler is dead. The Brock Report can be brought

out of the cupboard again. But the real question is, whether it is scientific. Let us, as in the case of abortion, ask the appropriate experts. Henderson and Gillespie, in their well-known *Textbook of Psychiatry,* say of the Brock Report:

> The above proposals are not only extremely wide but extremely vague and they create the paradoxical situation that the mentally defective and mentally unsound persons, who in no other respect can care for themselves, are supposed to be able to arrange for their own destiny, voluntarily, so far as steriliza-tion is concerned . . . In any case the possi-bility of exterminating mental deficiency by means of sterilization is well-nigh hopeless, as nine-tenths of the parents of defectives possess an intelligence within normal limits . . . It is unwise to accept what some euge-nists term neuropathic or psychopathic, and to regard a history of psychoneuroses, of insanity and of apoplexy in a family as con-stituing a bad heredity: the very salt of the earth may spring from such a stock.[212]

J. B. S. Haldane, F.R.S., is a scientist who suffers from none of the "irrational" religious prejudices that so irritate Dr. Glanville Williams. His conclu-sions are, therefore, specially pertinent. He exam-ined the arguments for eugenic sterilization in 1938, in his book *Heredity and Politics.*[213] Speaking as a biologist, he sweeps aside the alleged scientific argu-ments of the eugenists:

I think that the following proposition would be accepted by most biologists: "It is never possible, from a knowledge of a person's parents, to predict with certainty that he or she will be either a more adequate or a less adequate member of society than the majority."[214]

He examines a model Sterilization Law, drafted by an American eugenist, which would impose sterilization on "socially inadequate persons," including the feeble-minded and insane; the criminalistic, including the delinquent and wayward; the inebriate, including drug addicts; the diseased (those with chronic infections and legally segregable diseases, including tuberculosis); the blind, the deaf or seriously hard of hearing; the deformed, including the crippled; and finally, the dependent, including orphans, ne'er-do-wells, the homeless, tramps and paupers. On this, Professor Haldane is content to remark that its scope would include Milton (blind) and Beethoven (deaf).[215] He estimates that to prevent the birth of one child destined to schizophrenia in the next generation, we must sterilize about sixteen schizophrenics and prevent the birth of ten normal children.[216]

He notes a recurrent class bias in eugenist propaganda. In 1910 the Eugenics Society was advocating the sterilization of the unemployed.[217] He suspects that eugenism is an alibi for refusal of social and economic justice to the poor; he thinks that it enshrines "the doctrine of the innate superiority of

the children of the well-to-do."[218] We recall Dr.
Glanville Williams's revealing phrases, "upper
stratum . . . well-off and intelligent," and "lower
and uneducated classes . . . under-educated and
poverty-stricken groups."[219] We shall look in a
moment at more evidence of the class bias of contemporary eugenics.

On the moral issue, Professor Haldane concluded:

> To the majority of people, marriage means a
> great deal more than legalized sexual inter-
> course without the possibility of procreation,
> and any course of action which reduces it to
> that level appears to be at least as anti-social
> as one which allows an occasional defective
> to be born . . .[220] It is at least arguable that
> the proposal to turn out a number of mental
> defectives into the bitter economic struggles
> of modern life, provided only that they can-
> not reproduce, is a step morally backwards,
> and an abandonment of one of the forms of
> behaviour which distinguish man from most
> other animals.[221]

But these things will not cast a shadow of doubt
over Dr. Glanville Williams's faith. He knows the
"serious doubts" of geneticists already and feels
them as "a serious set-back for eugenic proposals."[222] But anyhow, he pleads, normal children
are better not reared by defective parents; and sterilization is good for defectives in any event.[223] There
are other considerations:

The four considerable advantages found to result from the operation are the prevention of the birth of handicapped children, the promotion of family welfare through the limitation of size, the improvement of maternal health, and last and least, the saving of public funds.[224]

If sterilization can only reduce hereditary ills by a small proportion each year, the result may still be to benefit tens of thousands of persons in each generation, as well as to save the community the cost of their care.[225] One argument for surgical sterilization is that it is a necessary corollary of medical and social advances in other fields. We have evolved by natural selection, but, by keeping alive mentally and physically ill-equipped children, we are opposing natural selection. The logical deduction seems to be that, unless steps are taken to counteract this tendency, we shall as a race become progressively less fit.[226]

It is surely a date in British legal literature, when such sentiments can be uttered in a book which has been greeted, on the whole, with only choruses of praise. It is impossible not to note, in these passages, and not to be shocked by, Dr. Glanville Williams's references to the "saving of public funds." We feel that this unfortunate argument is forced upon him by the logic of eugenism. We have already seen the Eugenics Society pleading, in 1910, for the sterilization of the unemployed. In 1926, the President of the Society, Major Leonard Darwin, the son of Charles Darwin, proposed

> that a list should be kept of all persons who had been in receipt of public assistance continuously for a given period . . . The list should contain a record of the number of children in each family; and all parents on the list who had two or more children should be warned that no more should be allowed to appear, and of the consequences of a neglect of this warning. These consequences should be an immediate cessation of all public assistance . . . When this warning was found to have been neglected, another child having made its appearance, and when also the family was found to be leading an uncivilized life, all its members should be segregated in some suitable institution . . . (But) all couples should be released from detention, either if it seemed probable that they could re-establish themselves in decent surroundings without public assistance or if the man consented to be sterilized . . .[227]

Such are the logical implications of eugenist philosophy. We feel that any humane man who has been attracted to this philosophy, will, when faced with them, want to do his thinking again. For he is involved with a philosophy which subordinates human beings to public funds; which equates physical fitness with moral worth; which takes an animal

view of man. Dr. Glanville Williams writes, in a
passage we have already quoted:

> The community is burdened with an enor-
> mous number of unfit members . . . The
> propagation of poor stock is regarded by
> public opinion as neither a sin nor a crime
> against humanity . . . There is a striking
> contrast between human fecklessness in our
> own reproduction and the careful scientific
> improvement of other forms of life under
> man's control. No rose-grower, pigeon-fan-
> cier or cattle-buyer would behave as men do
> in their own breeding habits. "Imagine,"
> says Bertrand Russell, "the feelings of a
> farmer who was told that he must give all his
> bull calves an equal opportunity."[228]

We doubt whether, when Dr. Glanville Williams
re-reads this passage "in a cool hour," he can be
entirely happy about the view of man which it
implies.

The Reverend Mr. Fletcher sees the important
issue here as "the right of society to be clean and
safe and the right of every child to be sound of
mind and body"; and says:

> It is imposible to see how the principle of
> social justice . . . can be satisfied if the com-
> munity may not defend itself, and is forced
> to permit the continued procreation of
> feeble-minded or hereditarily diseased chil-
> dren. Sterilization in such cases is not solely
> a matter of commutative justice (or personal

control), but also of distributive justice (or State control) . . . There is too much clinical or empirical evidence to be seen in institutions for the feeble-minded, for example, to believe for a minute that personal integrity is being or could be realized in such places.[229]

Hitler had a way of ensuring that feeble-minded and diseased children and patients in mental hospitals should not be a burden on public funds urgently needed for more virile uses. Hitler is not dead so long as his ideas survive.[230] The closest parallel that we have found to these passages from our contemporary British and American humanists is in an article on "Racial Morality" published in 1937 in the once notorious *Schwarze Korps*. Here we read:

A morality based on the demands of life is unable to set up an unchangeable moral code, because the external flux of life necessitates a progressive internal readjustment . . . Therefore we say: "Everything is good that promotes vitality—in short, everything great, strong and beautiful; everything is wrong and immoral that sets up walls and barriers around the centre of vitality." This view comes at once into collision with a great number of ecclesiastical moral laws, e.g., the attitude of the Church towards the eugenic legislation of the State. A morality that justifies the unchecked procreation of

stock that is by heredity and therefore morally inferior, a morality that destroys the
work of the Creator by the breeding of ra-
cially degenerate offspring, cannot claim to
correspond to the moral order willed by the
Creator . . . Everything that serves the preservation of the nation is morally good; everything that in the slightest degree threatens
its vitality is wrong and abominable.[231]

The Catholic condemnation of sterilization is
nothing other than the defence of humanity against
Hitlerism; for there is no logical stopping place for
eugenists short of the evil philosophy and the
wicked practices of the Nazis. There exists no re-
pudiation of Nazism more resolute or more complete than that of the late Pope Pius XI in his
encyclical *Mit brennender Sorge,* issued in 1937, in
the days of Hitler's unchallenged might.[232] It is in
this context that we can take the true measure of
the Christian doctrine of natural law. It shows itself
here as the assertion of humanism against biologism
and racism; the defence of man's rights and dignity
and freedom against totalitarian tyranny.[233]

Nazism could not progress except by attempting
to destroy the "barriers" set up against it by an
"unchangeable moral code." It is profitable, at this
point, to reflect upon some remarkable confessions
made by the late Lord Keynes in a memoir, *My
Early Beliefs.* Recalling student days at Cambridge
at the beginning of the century, he writes:

We entirely repudiated a personal liability

on us to obey general rules. . . . (We were entirely opposed to) morals, conventions and traditional wisdom . . . (This attitude was) flimsily based . . . on an *a priori* view of what human nature is like, both our own and other people's, which was disastrously mistaken . . . We repudiated all versions of the doctrine of original sin, of there being insane and irrational springs of wickedness in most men. We were not aware that civilization was a thin and precarious crust . . . Our comments on life and affairs were bright and amusing but brittle . . . because there was no solid diagnosis of human nature underlying them.[234]

Some things at Cambridge do not seem to have changed. If the crust of civilization holds, it will be in spite of them.

[202] P. 77. "This matter," he goes on, "cannot be too strongly insisted on, because it is not generally understood, and a grasp of the physiological facts is necessary if the social and personal importance of sterilization is to be appreciated. . . . All that (the operation) does is to prevent sexual activities from bearing their normal fruit. In this it has the same effect as the use of efficient contraceptives." A footnote says that, in the case of women, libido may even be increased; cf. p. 98.

[203] P. 82. "It is this limitation upon the effectiveness of contraception that creates the need for both sterilization and abortion as subsidary means of family planning and of eugenic and population control. Abortion, though sometimes the only possible solution, is a costly and wasteful form of birth control; and besides, some women will not accept abortion . . . Sterilization settles the problem once for all."

204 Pp. 96-9; 104-8. This is "the troublesome area" in the whole business for Dr. Glanville Williams. He finds even the "purported scientific literature" on the subject still full of "irrational arguments" against it. The old-fashionedness of judges makes surgeons afraid; and nobody suffers except women who are not wealthy enough to "make it worth the surgeon's while to take the legal risks involved." Gynaecologists mostly require the spouse's consent and this "means that they will sometimes feel unable to act in the patient's best interests merely because of the opposition of the spouse" (p. 107). "Many people feel," he quotes, "that such control by one individual over another is hardly to be thought desirable, however orthodox it may appear to the legal mind; and it is frequently criticized by health and social workers who are thus prevented from giving a constructive service to mentally or physically handicapped clients" (pp. 107-8). The Reverend Mr. Fletcher writes: "There is an assumption running throughout all that is said in behalf of our point of view, and it should be put clearly. It is that sexual love is inherently good, not evil; and eppediently good, as a physical and psychological drive requiring normal satisfaction . . ." (p. 161).

205 P. 87.

206 "The most important matter in any community is to make a start, no matter on how limited a scale" (p. 94).

207 Cited by A. Bonnar, *The Catholic Doctor,* p. 112.

208 Glanville Williams, p. 93.

209 Op. cit., p. 93. The quite unscientific vagueness of their language will be noted. Compare: "We were increasingly impressed by the injustice of refusing to those who *have good grounds for believing that they may* transmit mental defect or disorder . . . the only effective means of escaping from a burden which they *have every reason to dread"* (ibid.). (Italics ours.)

210 These decreed compulsory sterilization for (1) inborn feeblemindedness; (2) schizophrenia; (3) manic-depressive states; (4) hereditary epilepsy; (5) Huntington's Chorea; (6) blindness; (7) deafness; (8) severe hereditary physical deformity; (9) severe alcoholism.

211 P. 85.

212 Op. cit., Seventh Edition, 1952 Oxford University Press,

pp. 50, 53. Referring to the Nazi laws, the same authors say (op. cit., p. 50): "A knowledge regarding hereditary transmission is assumed which does not exist." These criticisms have been made, and the genetic arguments for sterilization refuted, again and again. See, e.g., Bonnar, *The Catholic Doctor*, pp. 111-123; H. Robbins, *An Examination of Eugenics*, Burns Oates, London, 1930; McFadden, *Medical Ethics*, pp. 314-324; J. S. Cammack, *Moral Problems of Mental Defect*, Burns Oates, London ,1938, pp. 40-88; E. F. Healy, *Medical Ethics*, Loyola University Press, Chicago, 1956, pp. 298-306. The quibble about "voluntary" sterilization of mental defectives has been often exposed: see Bonnar, op. cit., pp. 120-1; Cammack, op. cit., pp. 87-8; also Halliday Sutherland, *Laws of Life*, Sheed & Ward, London, 1941, pp. 135-142.

[213] Allen & Unwin, London.

[214] Pp. 86-7.

[215] Pp. 16-17. The Reverend Mr. Fletcher writes: "Developig research has tended to show that many diseases—such as renal calculus, nephritis, uterine cancer and certain toxaemias of pregnancy—are not only infective or environmental in origin but may be due to an hereditary vulnerability as well . . ."; and he goes on to complain of the neglect of genetics in medical education! (op. cit., p. 169).

[216] Pp. 88-90. Father Bonnar (op. cit., pp. 117-120) points to what he rightly calls the "startling statistics" involved in eugenist proposals. In England and Wales there would be "1,640,000 persons at least who can immediately be marked down for the surgeon's knife." If we add "recessive carriers," we should have to increase the total to some 18,000,000 persons, or 44 per cent. of the population; or, making a generous allowance for overlapping of categories, we should be left with about 35 per cent. of the population having to be sterilized. Father McFadden (op. cit., p. 316) writes: "Although 80 per cent. of our mental deficiency may be coming into society through channels of hereditary, all but 10 per cent. of it is being passed on through persons who are 'carriers' of these traits. These 'carriers' give no evidence of mental deficiency and are not able to be detected. A sterilization programme, therefore, would not affect 72 per cent. of the hereditary mental deficiency and would have no influence

on mental deficiency which is the product of environmental factors . . . Two other investigators on this subject, Huet-krantz and Gunnar, state that it would taken ten generations (of sterilization) before the percentage of defectives would be reduced by one half of one per cent., and that the subsequent rate of decrease would be still slower." See also Cammack, op. dic., pp. 56-88. These studies are sufficient commentary on the celebrated dictum of Justice Holmes in the United State Supreme Court in 1927—a dictum earnestly repeated by both Dr. Glanville Williams and the Reverend Mr. Fletcher: "Three generations of imbeciles are enough" (see Glanville Williams, p. 84; Fletcher, p. 166.) They are a commentary too on Dr. Glanville Williams's words: "To allow the breeding of defectives is a horrible evil . . ." (p. 212).

[217] Pp. 18-20.

[218] P. 94; cf. pp. 98, 100-1.

[219] Pp. 73-4.

[220] P. 101. The operation carries at least some danger to life; and Haldane says (p. 81): "I am not at all convinced that the principle of the sanctity of human life may not be of somewhat more importance for the State in the long run than a reduction in the number of defectives of certain kinds." This is a masterpiece of meiosis!

[221] P. 103. He sees in it the danger of a new form of slavery (p. 101). It is incredible how the eugenists can have overlooked the terrible consequences, in terms of exploitation of themselves and of dangers to public morals, which could not fail to ensue from the presence in society of mental defectives and weak-minded persons known to be sterilized.

[222] Pp. 85-6.

[223] Pp. 86-8. "The second discovery was made by the sterilization states and is of a distinctly encouraging character. This is that sterilization is to the advantage of the person sterilized and at least in the case of females, is actually welcomed" (p. 87).

[224] P. 89.

[225] P. 92.

[226] P. 83. The "logical deduction" seems rather to be mass extermination of the "unfit," not sterilization.

[227] Quoted in Halliday Sutherland, op. cit., pp. 125-6.

228 P. 83. Compare the other passages quoted on pp. 12-13, and the quotation from Charles Darwin in n. 139, p. 66, supra.

229 Op. cit., p. 168. Anti-sterilizationists condemn children "to enter upon a tragic and frustrated existence in a world they cannot understand or cope with" (p. 168). This might have been an exact description of Sartrean or Saganesque or 'Beat Generation' youths: but they are usually from the *best* bourgeois families, of excellent genetic stock.

230 Sterilization, historically and logically, is inseparable from racism and the division of mankind into masters and slaves, Herrenvolk and Slavs. Romans castrated slaves "with the same ease and for the same reasons as a domestic animal": slaves were "pre-personal." See the *Cahiers Laennec* studies of castration which have been translated by Malachy G. Carroll and edited by Dom Peter Flood in *New Problems in Medical Ethics,* III, Mercier Press, Cork, 1955, pp. 3-33. This is brutally brought home to us in a recent novel about the slave-owners of Alabama a century ago—*Mandingo* by Kyle Onstott. A reviewer in the *Times Literary Supplement* (6 February, 1959) writes in connection with it: "As stud-farmers, they are kindly and humane; so humane that they can only continue their degrading business by pretending to themselves that slaves are not fellowmen. For this, an elaborate terminology has been devised: babies are suckers, children saplings, men and women bucks and wenches. To castrate a young man might be revolting; no one minds the cutting of a sapling." Both Dr. Glanville Williams and the Reverend Mr. Fletcher repeat the legend of Vatican castration of choir-boys: anyone who wishes the truth about this should consult *New Problems in Medical Ethics,* III, pp. 12-20.

231 See *The Persecution of the Catholic Church in the Third Reich,* Facts and Documents, E. trans., Burns Oates, London, 1942, pp. 459-460. It is interesting to correlate with this a paragraph written recently by Sir Julian Huxley: "Within a century, we should have amassed adequate knowledge of what could be done negatively to lighten the burden of inherited deficiency of mind or body which presses so cruelly on so many individual human beings and so heavily on evolving humanity as a whole, and postively to raise the en-

tire level of innate human possibilities and capacities. When this has happened, the working out of an effective and acceptable eugenic policy will be seen as not only an urgent but an inspiring task, and its political or theological obstruction as immoral."—*New Bottles for New Wine,* Chatto and Windus, London, 1957, p. 306.

232 The Pope had already outspokenly condemned the "real pagan worship of the State—the Statolatry" of Mussolini's Fascism in 1931, in the encyclical *Non abbiano bisogno.*

233 For the background to this historic encyclical see *The Persecution of the Catholic Church in the Third Reich.* Compare Cardinal Faulhaber, *Judaism, Christianity and Germany,* Advent sermons preached in St. Michael's, Munich, in 1933, E. trans., Burns Oates, London, 1934.

234 *Two Memoirs,* ed. by David Garnett, R. Hart-Davis, London, 1949. pp. 98-9, 102.

12

Artificial Insemination

The most significant fact about the literature advocating artificial insemination is that it derives from animal stud-farms the concepts and the norms which it utilizes for human paternity. Dr. Glanville Williams squarely faces the implications of his philosophy:

If the "human stud farm" produces a sufficient overplus of good, it can, at least on a utilitarian philosophy, be justified.[235]

Artificial-inseminationists are, however, coming to realize that veterinary language is a serious liability to their case. Human beings just cannot think of these sacred relationships in animal terms. It is vital for the future of the campaign that the brute realities be veiled in the silk-smooth words of hygiene and aesthetics and moral purity; for scientific humanists worry more about a "morbid guilt sense" than theologians do about guilt. The "cult of cosiness" is already incipiently served by the use of initials: "A.I.D.," "A.I.H.," could shock no one.[235a]

The recently-created word "foster-pregnancy" is undoubtedly clever. There will be more words of the
same comforting sort. The "cheer-and-smear" technique has, indeed, already made a good start.[236]
Dr. Glanville Williams contrasts the "morbid," "sectarian," "doctrinaire," religious "obsessions" of the
opponents of artificial insemination, with the "empirical and imaginative humanitarianism" of its
advocates; he makes light of "aesthetic" scruples
against a "clinical" procedure, and associates insemination with science and progressiveness and
modernity. He recognizes, of course, that the struggle for "progress" will be long and hard; but he is
not daunted.

> The exploitation of the invention to its full
> effect would certainly involve a revolution
> in our social and moral ideas, which is un-
> likely but not totally impossible.[237]

He starts by innocently pretending that he does
not understand what all the fuss is about.

> When the husband is sterile—when he has
> no sperm at all—he and his wife may buy
> some. This simple transaction has provoked
> strong objections, with demands for its sup-
> pression through the agency of the criminal
> law.[238]

This can be taken as the measure of the scientific
humanists' understanding either of science or of
human reality. To speak of sperm as something one
may buy or sell is an exhibition of ignorance. To
compare sperm with "any other part of the body,

e.g., hair," is disingenuous. To liken the semen-donor to the blood-donor, as inseminationists cleverly do,[239] is sophistry; it is the logical fallacy of false analogy. Even scientifically, semen is not just a bodily secretion. It is not merely one of man's anatomical or physiological constituents; it is the precondition of the existence of any human kind; it is the condition *sine qua non* of the existence of any human value. Semen takes its value from the value of man, its meaning from the meaning of man. The significance of semen merges into the significance of human existence itself. Semen is the carrier of man's inheritance and history, the transmitter of his name and race, his memory and his hopes. It belongs to him, not as an isolated individual, but as one indebted to the past and answerable for the future of humanity. If Dr. Glanville Williams will not heed "sacred writing and priestly pronouncements,"[240] let him at least listen to the psychologists: they all insist on the paramount influence of sexuality on human character and personality. His ideas are pre-Freudian!

But whereas Freud tended to speak as though spirit were the expression of sex, the truth is that sex is an expression of spirit.[241] It is inseverable from morality and values and religion. No use of sex is truly human or moral which does not respect man's spiritual nature. The emission of semen is under man's control; and therefore engages his moral responsibility. It is an act which expresses his respect or disrespect for the human, in himself and in another. One respects the human, sexually, only in the institutions of marriage and the family. One respects the human in the use of semen, only when it is transmitted from husband to wife in an act of marriage which expresses their "worship" ("worthship") of body and spirit for each other. An attitude to semen is an evaluation of man. What one does with semen, one will do with man.[242] The language of buying and selling semen is at home only in a culture which accepts the buying and selling of men. The Romans, who had no cult of verbal cosiness, show us the logic of this language. Slaves, for them, were beings *in quos stuprum non committitur;* because they were *things,* not persons. A prostitute was a *prostibulum,* a *thing* displayed for sale. It is perhaps the cruellest word in history. In a sense, all immorality is the treating of persons as *things.* In that sense, treating semen as a *thing* is an incarnation of immorality and a prelude to an inhuman society.[243]

What must be emphasized in discussing this subject is that it is not question of a particular clinical technique;[244] it is equivalently a whole new philosophy and metaphysics of man, a new morality, a total anti-religion. Dr. Glanville Williams writes:

Artificial insemination does offer some slight hope of improving human strains. It opens the way for separating the procreative from the companionate and sexual elements in marriage. A woman can now choose one man as the biological father of her children

and another as her lover and companion,
and as the father of her children by adoption. It offers the possibility, too, of im-
mensely increasing the number of women
whom it is praticable for one man, regarded
as of good stock, to fertilize.[245]

This means that, purely and simply, the notion of
fatherhood and of family are being abolished. To
abolish these is both to dehumanize man and to
deny God.

The Reverend Mr. Fletcher argues, in favour of
test-tube paternity, that it is only "an impersonal
procedure of medical technology";[246] that a donor
acts only "in a scientific and purely impersonal
spirit";[247] that the donor-father's children are "his"
"only in a most materialistic and natural sense."[248]
He is trying to defend insemination against the
charges of adultery by arguing that, whereas adultery is a personal relationship, semen-donating is
not.[249] All moral objections to artificial insemination
are answered according to him by the fact that "no
personal relationship is entered into with the donor
at all."[250] Long-distance transportation, organization, on a national scale, of semen-banks, all this
eliminates the personal factor from paternity entirely.[251] Dr. Glanville Williams, too, is impressed
with the praeter-human dimensions which insemination gives to procreation.

The way is open for semen banks to be built
up, supplying semen methodically classified
as to the characteristics of the donor. Such

semen could, of course, be used years after
the donor is dead.[252]

It is important to realize that even this is only
a beginning. It is not only semen which can be do-
nated; it will undoubtedly, we are told, become
possible to "(transplant) fertilized ova from one
female to another" so that the foster-mother can
"bear a child which is biologically the child of the
donor and has no characteristics of the foster-
mother." Women could thus "have" children without "bearing" them.[253] With the abolition of the
family, population policy can really become both
scientific and strategic, as was noted at an American
symposium by one of "the world's leading geneticists," Dr. Hermann J. Muller:

Foster pregnancy, which is already possible,
will become socially acceptable and even socially obligatory. It will seem wrong to breed
children who mirror parents' pecularities
and weaknesses. In the future children will
be produced by the union of ovum and
sperm, both derived from persons of proved
worth, possibly long deceased, who exem-
plify the ideals of the foster-parents. The
first nation to do this will be able to breed a
race which will be so superior that it will
dominate the rest.[254]

Bertrand Russell foresaw these possibilities
when he wrote *The Scientific Outlook* in 1931.
Aldous Huxley imagined a society in which these
techniques were standard practice, in his *Brave New*

World in 1932. The public was more amused than shocked by these writings, which they read as horrific science-fiction or as macabre humour. The techniques themselves were seen as shocking; the idea that they might ever become serious policy seemed merely amusing. But twenty-five years later, not novelists or prophets of doom, but scientists, lawyers and parsons are calmly defending these techniques as morally good and are advocating their legislative recognition in the name of human progress. These ideas have moved from the realm of science-fiction into that of scientific symposium and legal seminar.

It is incomprehensible how inseminationists can, in one context, condemn Catholic sexual morality as impersonal and biologistic or reproductionist, and in another, themselves argue that reproduction by insemination is moral *because* it is merely impersonal and biological and materialistically reproductive. Our case against artificial insemination is precisely that it *is* impersonal. Human moral values are safeguarded only at the level of the personal; therefore, human beings, the trustees of all moral values, may be brought into existence only at the level of the personal. A human person can be begotten in a moral, that is in a human way, only by a personal act of love. Artificial insemination is evil because procreation is never merely a biological process. A man cannot morally be a father in a "merely materialistic" sense, because a child is not a material thing.

The fatal fallacy of inseminationist reasoning is
to suppose that having a child or being a father are
matters of mere physical gestating or animal "sir-
ing." But nothing in man is merely physical or animal: the physical in man is inhabited by spirit; and
when it does not respect the spirit, it is, not animal,
but perverse spirit, that is to say, diabolic. Fatherhood or motherhood, in particular, is a spiritual
relationship incarnated in a physical relationship,
and these are inseparable, as body is from soul.
Paternity is a work of love, of the physical-spiritual
love of a man for the mother of his child; of the
physical-spiritual love of man and woman for the
child in whom they recognize and love the oneness
of their flesh. Artificial insemination sunders flesh
from spirit; and turns, like manicheism, into contempt of both.

Fatherhood is not an act or a reflex; not a service or a function. It is unbelievable that humanists
can suppose that a human father's role is fulfilled
by an act of routine self-abuse; and that he is
thenceforth free from all responsibility or care or
thought for the offspring of his seed. They see the
need, however, for precautions to protect the parties against disturbance from the natural human instincts that are implicated with procreation. Dr.
Glanville Williams says:

It is the invariable rule of physicians . . . to
keep the identity of the donor an absolute
secret even from the husband and wife, and
conversely to keep from the donor all knowl-

edge of the family into which his genes will enter. Among the reasons for this secrecy are the desire to protect the donor's reputation (think of the repercussions for his family if his adventures in paternity became common gossip!) and to eliminate the risk of the donor blackmailing the couple, as well as the risk of the wife transferring her affection to the donor. For all these reasons . . . some physicians make a practice of keeping no records of the transaction.[255]

Even from the point of view of instinct, fatherhood cannot be separated from love; it spontaneously arouses both paternal love and conjugal love. Fatherhood means loving a new life, a new person, into manhood. It is never a mere biological process. A man "fathers" his child all his life long; otherwise his child is a deprived child, an "unwanted child." The very people whom we have seen pleading so passionately for "voluntary parenthood" are now found, in another context, endorsing absentee parenthood, in which it is deliberately ensured that the father will never even want to know who his children are, or the woman, who was her mate. The very people who have such pity for the "unwanted child" are here insisting that the child shall never even know who his father was or who it is whose physical likeness and psychological traits he inherits.[256]

Sociologists and psychologists emphasize more and more every year the role of paternal and ma-

ternal deprivation in the aetiology of juvenile delinquency. Social studies and statistics reveal the circle which leads from illegitimate birth to deprivation
of paternal-maternal affection and from that to
emotional disturbance, insecurity, maladjustment,
delinquency and back to illegitimate parenthood,
where the tragic round begins again.[257] One knows
enough of the dejection and distress of young people when they discover that their parents were not
married and that their father would not own them
and their mother could not or would not rear them.
How shall we picture the anguish of a young person
when he discovers that even his mother does not
know who gave him life within her? Let lawyers
discuss as they will whether the A.I.D. child is
civilly illegitimate or not; from the moral and human point of view the process is worse than illegitimacy. There is something human even in the weakness and wickedness of sinful love. The father of an
illegitimate child has had, for a time, at least a
simulacrum of love for a woman. The semen-donor
has loved no one—except perhaps his own physical
strength.[258]

It is indeed strange that inseminationists, in their
enthusiastic advocacy of superman-sires, have failed
to consider the effects on the character of the donor
who accepts his designation and function as a
Superman. There is no worse sin than spiritual
pride. There is no greater manifestation of pride
than to believe in one's moral superiority to one's
fellow-men; and, in the new eugenist society, physi-

cal fitness will be the criterion of moral worth. Here we touch upon the fundamental vice of this sort of scientific humanism it identifies physical health and strength with moral excellence. There is surely no need to call attention again to the trite "naturalistic fallacy," so frequently pointed out to evolutionist moralists, which is involved in confusing biological "fitness" with moral "fitness." To make this confusion is to range oneself with the pernicious myths of Blood and Soil and Master Race. It is to return from morality to barbarism. Camus—a tuberculosis victim who would certainly not be allowed to be a father, and would perhaps not have been allowed to be born, in a eugenic society—has spoken of "the miserable powers of today, which can destroy but cannot convince."[259] One has been convinced of man's true excellence more by seeing how good men suffer than by seeing how strong men succeed. One has learnt more about what man is and how he becomes good, from visiting the wards of hospitals than from following the athletic triumphs of the well-built males who would pass the tests for fitness to be A.I. donors.[260]

The consequences of artificial insemination within the conjugal circle are no less grave. Nothing can so undermine a personality as a sense of inferiority. The A.I.D. child in a home will be a permanent reminder to the sterile husband of his inferiority and impotence.[261] The child, which should be a bond and pledge of union, not only of two bodies, but of two personalities, has instead become a barrier of division, a proof of inequality, a threat to the stability of the marriage.[262]

It is impossible not to fear that the spread of inseminationist mentality would have the effect of extending the area of psychological propensity towards homosexuality. There is no doubt about the preponderant role in the aetiology of homosexuality played by mother-dominance and by psychological narcissism. A child who owes his birth and heredity to his mother only, and who has no kinship with his legal "father," will be hard to safeguard from the mother-dominance which is held to account for eighty per cent. of homosexuality.[263] A semen-donor, conscious of his mascuuline pre-eminence, will find it difficult to avoid the narcissistic egoism which, is the supreme characteristic of homosexuals.[264]

There is, however, a really frightening determination on the part of inseminationists to let no consequence however immoral deflect them from their objective. It is as though they were forced, by the logic of their position, into abandoning all moral sense and standards. Firstly, they are forced to condone fraud and deception on the part of both parent and doctor. We have already quoted Dr. Glanville Williams' insistence on the need for secrecy. He goes on:

> For all these reasons . . . some physicians make a practice of keeping no records of the transaction. Others, however, keep records, and where they do, there is a slight risk that

the secrecy of the transaction may be broken
by the physician being subpoenaed to give
evidence. . . . Another disadvantage (of
adoption procedure for the A.I. child) is
that since adoption requires consent of the
child's natural parent, an inquiry would have
to be made into the identity of the donor,
which it is the whole object of medical practice to suppress.[265]

For these reasons, he urges that legislation
should be passed to legitimize children born of
A.I.D. with the husband's consent; but he does not
say how, in that case, the other risks he has men-
tioned on the preceding page (of the donor's blackmailing the couple or of the woman's transferring
her affection to the donor) are to be avoided.

Most doctors who campaign for A.I.D. seem to
have little scruple in recommending secrecy, backed
up by lies. A French doctor insists that the secret
must be guarded absolutely from the child, who
must be allowed to have no doubt about his origin;
and endorses the practice of having the delivery of
the child effected by a different doctor (from the
one who performed the insemination), "who will be
able to sign the birth-certificate without mental reservation."[266] The two legal members of the Archbishop of Canterbury's Commission[267] recorded
their surprise at reading in an article in the *British
Medical Journal*[268] that:

the couple are informed that the child will
be legitimate if the husband is registered as

the father; such registration is demanded,
although it constitutes an offence.

They point out that this is to make the medical
practitioner "the instigator of and accessory to the
crime" of "making a false and fradulent record"
of birth.[269] A practice which requires doctors to lie
and to justify lying should need nothing more to
condemn it in the eyes of the honourable medical
profession. The Archbishop of Canterbury's Commission declared:

> To confer on a child the name of a putative
> father and allow him to grow up in ignor-
> ance of the real relationship between them
> is—whatever the motives which prompt it—
> to be guilty of fraud.[270]

It is surely one of the most cruel frauds one could
perpetrate on a human being—a lie about his name
and identity. For those responsible it is very close
to the "lie in the soul"; not a lie one tells, but a lie
one lives and is.

Adoption is summarily dismissed by these eugenists as failing to meet the emotional and biological needs of childless couples. But adoption has the
incomparable advantage over artificial insemination
that it does not need to hide or fear the truth; and
that it represents a shared decision, and is a work
of shared love between two equal partners. Marriage
binds a man and a woman to love each the other
as his or her own body. It is fundamentally incompatible with marriage that either partner should
realize his or her natural desire to procreate chil-

dren otherwise than through their oneness in one flesh. A woman does not desire just to "acquire" a child; she desires to "be given" a child by the man she loves. She wants, not just *a* child, not even "a child of her own," but "*his* child."[271] If she loves him, she will rather remain childless than cause him the hurt and humiliation of bearing a child which is not his. A parent does not say "my children" but "our children." A mother is just as likely to say "his children"; and to refer to her husband as "the children's father." These are the deep and precious human things which artificial insemination would destroy.

Inseminationists know, of course, that such means as lying are wrong. But their philosophy commits them to the view that wrong becomes right when done in a good cause. This is made very clear by their attitude to masturbation. Dr. Glanville Williams seems to hesitate between the view that masturbation is morally unobjectionable, provided it is "done without feelings of guilt" due to "morbid religious obsession"; and the view that, objectionable though it is in itself, it is justified by the good end of relieving barrenness in other people's marriages.[272] The Reverend Mr. Fletcher, with his usual lack of subtlety, makes the point quite clear:

> Even if we grant that masturbation is self-abuse when practised for its own sake, does it not lose that character when it becomes the method or means to a procreative purpose which is otherwise impossible?[273]

The point to note here is that there is no tyranny or inhumanity or wickedness in history, or on the earth today, but which claims to be justified by precisely this principle. Camus has called it "the golden rule of the contemporary mind, that one cannot make omelettes without breaking eggs."[274]

The Reverend Mr. Fletcher is much too tender-hearted to hurt anyone; but it is amazing how tough-minded he can be in accepting the most extreme consequences of his ethical premises. It has been frequently pointed out that one donor could produce enormous numbers of children.[275] This, combined with the practice of concealment of fatherhood and falsification of birth certificates, clearly creates "a grave danger of widespread incest."[276] The prospect is appalling. But the Reverend Mr. Fletcher is not appalled. From the standpoint of genetic science, where he stands,

> in-breeding is not known to be genetically harmful except among stocks which are too poor to stand an accentuation of their qualities, or characteristic lack of them.

This language is somewhat difficult for the non-scientist to grasp! But there is no ambiguity about what follows:

> If people seeking A.I.D. choose to be scientific in their reasoning, and prefer to discount the danger of incest as a possible consequence, who is to find any ethical objection?[277]

Our Reverend Professor of Christian Ethics dares

to be bolder yet, just to prove, presumably, that nothing can shock a Modern Churchman.

> If . . . we are not content to accept the legalistic and naturalistic assumption . . . then there seems to be no good reason for objecting to A.I.D. for unmarried mothers . . . The practice may well be disapproved on other grounds, such as the alleged inability of women to bring up children without a male helpmeet. But this is an admitted objection to motherhood in the case of widows and grass-widows too. Yet is it not true that one parent is better than none?[278]

In fact, however, what artificial insemination ideology means is not the making redundant of one parent, but the abolition of the very meaning of human parenthood as such. It is the sacred name of Father that is being subverted.[279] The inseminationist is proposing that a child shall never be able to call any *person* "My father." He is proposing that that child shall never know, as a personal truth, what fatherhood means. Let us try the experiment of eliminating one by one the experiences, the loves, the loyalties, the values, which we can name only by using the word "father," alone or with suffixes— then we shall have an idea of the brutishness to which "scientific reproduction" would reduce humanity.

Nor is it only human fatherhood that is marked down for destruction; it is also, and indeed primarily, the Fatherhood of God, the very notion of

God, which is being eliminated. God Himself could
find no better name to express His Being and His
creating and loving relation to mankind than the
human name of Father. Who strikes at human
fatherhood strikes at God.[280] Freud's theory of religion, crude though its errors are, has at least the
merit of emphasizing the importance in religion of
the notion and the experience of fatherhood. But it
is not, as he shallowly supposes, that the idea of
God is the projection of the human idea of father.
Rather is it from the idea and self-revelation of
God as Father that we learn what human fatherhood should be. God's is the fatherhood of whom
all fatherhood in heaven and on earth is named.
Because it prevents fatherhood, artificial insemination is not merely a technique to be pronounced
morally wrong: it is anti-moral, anti-man and anti-
God.

Dr. Glanville Williams and the Reverend Mr.
Fletcher both attach much importance to the question of whether A.I.D. is or is not adultery. The
Cambridge lawyer's discussion is vitiated by his in-
ability—which is, of course, a grave defect of his
whole book—to distinguish legal from moral and
theological concepts and to confine himself to the
legal aspects in which, as a lawyer, he has competence. He writes:

> To sum up, although it is possible for the
> moral meaning of adultery to differ from the
> legal one, there is no realistic way in which
> A.I.D. performed with the husband's con-

sent can be said to be adultery in morals,
even if it is adultery in law.[281]

A theologian cannot claim to know as much
about law as Dr. Glanville Williams claims to know
about morals and theology. He does not, however,
make the mistake of identifying law and morals, or
crime and sin. He leaves to the lawyers the argument as to whether or not A.I.D. is legally to be
classed as adultery: it is matter in large part of legal
definition and interpretation.[282] From the moral
point of view, no doubt is possible: donor insemination possesses the full moral species of adultery,
going beyond "ordinary" adultery, however, in
moral turpitude, because it is more unnatural and
inhuman.[283] The "impersonal" character of insemination, which is urged by its supporters in its defence, is indeed, as we have seen, the chief reason
for its moral condemnation. As Pope Pius XII said:

To consider the cohabitation of husband and
wife and the marital act as a simple organic
function for the transmission of seed, would
be the same as to convert the domestic
hearth, which is the family sanctuary, into a
mere biological laboratory . . . The marital
act, in its natural setting, is a personal action. It is the simultaneous and direct co-
operation of husband and wife which, by the
very nature of the agents and the propriety
of the act, is the expression of the mutual
giving which, in the words of Scripture, results in the union "in one flesh." This is

much more than the union of two life-germs,
which can be brought about even artificially,
that is without the co-operation of the husband and wife. The marital act, in the order
of nature and by the design of nature, consists of a personal co-operation which the
husband and wife exchange as a right when
they marry.[284]

Here, as always, the doctrine of natural law is the
assertion of man's transendence over biological and
physico-chemical nature. It is the defence of man
against the sub-human.

[235] Op. cit., p. 134.

[235a] The initials, of course, stand for "Artificial Insemination
by a Donor," "Artificial Insemination by the Husband," re-
spectively.

[236] No chapter of Dr. Glanville Williams's book is so full of
emotive smear-and-cheerwords as the chapter on Artificial
Insemination. "Have no fear," boasts the Reverend Mr.
Fletcher, for his part, "it will be found that there are plenty
of twentieth-century wives. The testimony of physicians
shows it" (p. 129).

[237] P. 113.

[238] P. 110. Later, referring to some legal and other objections and difficulties he dismisses them impatiently as mere
"matters of detail" (pp. 136-8).

[239] See op. cit., p. 134; cf. Fletcher, op. cit., p. 120.

[240] P. 126.

[241] We have developed this theme on earlier pages (see pp.
41-53). It is worth while to quote here again the words of
Sartre (from "Questions de Methode," in *Les Temps Modernes,* CXXXX, Sept. 1957, p. 381): "Sexuality is only a
way of living, at a certain level and in the perspective of a
certain individual adventure, the totality of our human condition."

[242] Compare the reflections of Gabriel Marcel in the sympo-

sium *L'insemination Artificielle,* Centre d'Etudes Laennec, Lethielleux, Paris, pp. 35-46. This has been translated in *New Problems in Medical Ethics,* II, ed. by Dom Peter Flood, Mercier Press, Cork, 1957, pp. 3-58.

243 Bertrand Russell saw that it logically entailed tyranny; one of the most foolish things he ever said was: "Nevertheless, if there is to be tyranny, it is better that it should be scientific" (*Marriage and Morals,* p. 214). He has repented of this long ago.

244 "An interesting medico-social experiment," Glanville Williams calls it (p. 115).

245 Pp. 112-3; compare Julian Huxley, in *The Uniqueness of Man:* "It is now open to man and woman to consummate the sexual function with those they love but to fulfil the reproductive with those whom on perhaps quite other grounds they admire . . . (But) . . . it is first necessary to overcome the bitter opposition to it on dogmatic theological and moral grounds . . . Unless we alter the social framework of law and ideas, so as to make possible the divorce between sex and reproduction . . . our efforts at evolutionary improvement will remain mere tinkering." Cited in *Artificial Human Insemination,* Report of Commission appointed by His Grace the Archbishop of Canterbury, S.P.C.K., London, 1948, p. 8. Compare Russell, *Marriage and Morals,* pp. 133, 211, 238, on the separation of sex from reproduction. The Reverend Mr. Fletcher sees, as opposed to A.I.D., "the assumptions of the present philosophy of law and parenthood" (p. 137).

246 P. 121.

247 P. 129.

248 Ibid.; cf. p. 139.

249 Pp. 118-129.

250 P. 121. Bertrand Russell in *The Scientific Outlook,* Allen & Unwin, London (1931), 1954, prophesied: "Perhaps it will be found that artificial insemination is more certain and less embarrassing, since it will obviate the need of any personal contact between the father and mother of the porspective child . . . (Impregnation) will be regarded in an entirely different manner (from intercourse not intended to be fruitful), more in the light of a surgical operation, so that it will

be thought not ladylike to have it performed in the natural manner" (p. 263).

[251] Fletcher, op. cit., pp. 128-9: "It is a fairly easily worked out arrangement in the medical services, over a wide area of co-operation and exchange." He argues that "the practice of local donations could be dropped altogether," and seminal fluid shipped to great distances.

[252] P. 114. It seems that two such "semen-banks" already exist, one in New York and one in Iowa. It is claimed that there are about 100,000 "test-tube babies" in the United States.

[253] Ibid. Dr. Glanville Williams is only noting the possibilities; for the present he discusses the legal and moral problems only of insemination.

[254] See *The Observer,* 24 November, 1957. Dr. Muller received the Nobel Prize for his work on radiation and hereditary endowment. Bertrand Russell predicted that the fetus, during gestation, "would be subjected to various kinds of scientific treatment intended to affect beneficially not only its own characteristics but those of its possible descendants" —*The Scientific Outlook,* p. 263. Compare Dr. Glanville Williams, pp. 94-5: "There is every reason to expect a day when a man's genetic constitution will be able to be determined otherwise than by the trial-and-error method of waiting for him to sire children and grandchildren. When genes can be docketed under the microscope, the prospect of a vast improvement in the human race will, given the willingness to work for it, become a reality." Jean Rostand, one of the best known research-workers in this field, has surveyed the prospects for "scientific improvement" of man in his *Peut-on modifier l'homme?* He concludes his survey of the possibilities of producing a race of biological Supermen by writing. "There is only one way for man to raise himself up, to make himself greater, to become "more-a-man"—and that is by generosity, devotedness and the gift of self." *Peut-on modifier l'homme,* Gallimard, Paris, 1956, p. 143.

[255] P. 117. Both Dr. Glanville Williams (p. 124) and the Reverend Mr. Fletcher (pp. 136-7) praise a 1949 law of Ontario whereby all children born to a married woman are registered in her name, no indication of paternity being given. The Reverend Mr. Fletcher comments: "Under this

law A.I.D. children are given a better break in terms of reactionary attitudes . . . Without entering into the whole
question of whether there is ethically such a thing as an
illegitimate child, we should be clear that the Ontario law
makes a step forward in moral growth." See Biot, *Offensives
biologiques contre la personne,* Spes, Paris, 1949, pp. 176-7,
and generally pp. 140-178.

[256] Jean Lacroix, in *Force et faiblesses de la famille,* stresses
the profound meaning and importance in human history of
the recognition and acceptance by the father of the child as
"his child" (see pp .58 ff.).

[257] See, for example, the World Health Organization Mono-
graphs, *Maternal Care and Mental Health,* by J. Bowby,
Geneva, 1952 (especially the chapters on "The Purpose of
the Family" and "The Causes of Family Failure in Western
Communities"); and *Psychiatric Aspects of Juvenile Delinquency* by L. Bovet, Geneva, 1951, especially the chapter on
"Etiology." Compare E. de Greeff, *Our Children and Ourselves,* E. Trans., Clonmore and Reynolds, Dublin, 1958,
esp. pp. 14-15, 34, 42.

[258] "Most of the donors in the United States and Canada,"
says the Reverend Mr. Fletcher, "are medical students and
internes who respond to appeals for donations in a scientific
and purely impersonal spirit." In America, it is found prefer-
able that there should be a nominal payment, according to
Dr. Glanville Williams (p. 134).

[259] In his Nobel Prize speech of 1957, published in *Discours
de Suède,* Gallimard, Paris, 1958, p. 17.

[260] For the qualities of donors see, e.g., *Artificial Human Insemination,* p. 33; *L'Insemination Artificielle,* p. 19; Dr.
Glanville Williams, pp. 121-2.

[261] Compare *L'Insemination Artificielle,* p. 41; *Artificial Human Insemination,* pp. 24-8.

[262] It is significant that inseminationists insist that, before
performing an insemination-operation, a doctor should first
satisfy himself that the marriage in question is a stable one:
see *L'insemination Artificielle,* p. 21. The Reverend Mr.
Fletcher remarks (p. 126): "The insights of marital coun-
selling make it clear that A.I.D. should never be undertaken
to save a crumbling marriage. It is sound only for couples
who are well and truly married."

263 See *Les états intersexuels* (Centre d'études Laennec), Lethielleux, Paris, 1950, pp. 55-6. This has been translated in *New Problems in Medical Ethics,* I, ed. by Dom Peter Flood, Mercier Press, Cork, 1953.

264 *Les états intersexuels,* pp. 102-3, 107, 112. In an impressive study, "De Platon à Gide," J. Gengoux traces the effects, in Greek and in modern society, of the separation of heterosexual love from procreation. The effect is, on the one hand, to take away the seriousness of the hetero-sexual relations and turn the love of man and woman into pleasure-seeking play and pastime; and, on the other, to accentuate the masculinity of society and to give prestige to homosexual relationships (op. cit., 68-95). Very similar conclusions, from a totally different starting point, are arrived at by Bertrand Russell: see, e.g., his chapter "Scientific Reproduction," in *The Scientific Outlook.* For the element of "egolatry" in homosexuality, see Ch. Larère in *Les états intersexuels,* pp. 101-7. Ultimately, he says, for the homosexual, "I am God." This, interestingly, is a main charge of Sartre against the homosexual Jean Genet: see *Saint Genet, Comédian et Martyr,* Gallimard, Paris, 1952, p. 176 et saepe.

265 Pp. 117-8.

266 Doctor Palmer, of the Gynaecological Department of the Paris Faculty of Medicine, in *L'insemination Artificielle,* pp. 20-24.

267 The Hon. Mr. Justice H. B. Vaisey, D.C.L., and the Right Hon. H. V. Willink, M.C., K.C.

268 1945, i, 40.

269 *Artificial Human Insemination,* p. 40; compare pp. 15-17, 26, 31, 34-5, 52-3. It must be recorded, to the Reverend Mr. Fletcher's credit, that he cannot stomach lies in this matter: the parents, he declares, should frankly tell the child that it has been "co-opted"! (pp. 126-7).

270 P. 53.

271 Cf. *L'Insemination Artificielle,* pp. 88-90; S. de Lestapis, *Amour et Institution Familiale,* pp. 134-140.

272 Pp. 131-4.

273 P. 118; cf. p. 138. The Archbishop of Canterbury's Commission, whose standpoint on the morality of A.I.D. is generally admirable, unfortunately falls into the fatal error of allowing that masturbation by a husband may be morally

good *if* intended for the fecundation of his wife: "Many will hold that in this event, and as a last resource, masturbation may be legitimate. The act . . . being in this instance directed towards the completion (impossible without it) of the procreative end of the marriage, loses its character of self-abuse. It cannot, on this view, be the will of God that a husband and wife should remain childless merely because an act of this kind is required to promote conception"—(op. cit., p. 47). The tragedy is that, if this principle (that something evil in itself loses its evil character if done for a good end) is conceded, it becomes impossible to pronounce A.I.D. itself to be morally evil.

[274] *Discours de Suède*, p. 50.

[275] On one calculation, 400 children weekly, or about 20,000 annually: see *Artificial Human Insemination,* p. 10; cf. Glanville Williams, pp. 117, 133-4; Biot, *Offensives biologiques,* etc., pp. 169-171.

[276] Fletcher, p. 130.

[277] Pp. 129-131.

[278] Pp. 130-1. His argument is that artificial insemination is not an interpersonal relationship between a man and a woman and therefore cannot constitute fornication or adultery. "If," he goes on, "there is any real objection . . . it must be to unmarried motherhood itself. Whether it is possible to defend a doctrine that confines parenthood absolutely to marriage (whether polygamous, polyandrous or group marriage) is a question in social ethics that lies outside our scope" (pp. 131-2). Earlier he had quoted, without disapproval, the opinion of Dr. Frances Seymour, medical director of Eugenic Alleviation of Sterility, Inc., who says she "has given 'laboratory babies' to many unmarried as well as married women." "It is every woman's heritage," she declares, "to bear children. A.I. provides the unmarried business woman with a decent and moral method of acquiring the children nature intended her to bear" (pp. 103-4). We do not doubt that Dr. Frances Seymour and her collaborators, when they have time off from their duties in Eugenic Alleviation of Sterility, Inc., are zealous supporters of the Planned Parenthood Federation of America in its efforts to provide *married* women with methods to *avoid* acquiring the children nature intended them to bear!

279 See the reflections of Gabriel Marcel, in *L'insemination Artificielle,* pp. 35-46; and his chapters, "Le mystère familial," and "Le voeu créateur comme essence de la paternité" in *Homo Viator,* Aubier, Paris, 1944; cf. *Du refus à l'invocation,* La Colombe, Paris, 1951, pp. 35-38, 122 ff.

280 See the remarkable chapter of Jean Lacroix, "Le meurtre du père," in *Force et faiblesses de la famile,* in which he reflects on the extent to which modern atheism may be seen as bound up with—in the words of Kafka—"an attempt to escape from the sphere of the father" (pp. 13-44).

281 P. 131.

282 The legal experts on the Archbishop of Canterbury's Commission had "no doubt at all that the act both of a married donor and a married recipient constitutes adultery" and that the offspring is illegitimate. See op. cit., pp. 37-41 and cf. p. 47. They conclude: "This is not a matter in which the law ought to interfere otherwise than by prohibiting A.I.D. altogether . . . In our view the evils necessarily involved in A.I.D. are so grave that early consideration should be given to the framing of legislation to make the practice a criminal offence" (p. 42). This was the recommendation of the entire Commission with the single exception of the Very Rev. W. R. Matthews, the Dean of St. Paul's. The Dean's theology, as revealed in his Note (pp. 59-63), is not notably different from that Reverend Mr. Fletcher; or indeed from that of Dr. Glanville Williams.

In a recent Scottish case concerning A.I.D. without husband's consent, Lord Wheatley, while admitting that "grave moral, ethical, social and personal considerations" are involved, and while recognising that A.I.D. is a "grave and heinous offence of the contract of marriage," went on to declare that his problem as Judge was "not the moral culpability of such an act but whether it constituted adultery in its legal meaning." If it were not adultery but still a grave breach of the marriage contract, then, if a legal remedy were required, this was a matter for the legislature. But A.I.D., he found, "does not conform to the common conception of adultery." "Just as A.I. extracts procreation entirely from the nexus of human relations in or outside of marriage, so does the extraction of the nexus of human relations from the act of procreation remove A.I. from the classification of sexual intercourse." See *The Times,* 11 January, 1958.

[283] The Archbishop of Canterbury, writing to *The Times* on 15 January, 1958, said that, for the donor, A.I.D. is "far less responsible and far less human than adultery." He said that "either the practice of A.I.D. should be made a criminal offence altogether, or if that cannot be, then the law should require that every case of A.I.D. should be registered and the register should be available for inspection under safeguards." He urged that "legislation of some kind is urgently needed to resolve the doubts and to preserve under control the integrity of marriage and the family."

A British Home Office Committee, under the chairmanship of Lord Faversham, has recently concluded its investigation of artificial insemination and the law by rejecting proposals for the legalization of A.I.D. and recommending that the practice be strongly discouraged. There were only two dissentients. The Committee took the view, however, that A.I.D. should not be forbidden by law, on the grounds that the ban would be unenforceable. Church of England witnesses agreed with Catholic spokesmen that A.I.D. is fundamentally opposed to the Christian institution of marriage and is gravely injurious to society. Most Rev. Dr. Dwyer, Bishop of Leeds, in a comment, said that, if the total banning of A.I.D. was unenforceable, "at least the organizing of A.I.D. as a technique by banks of donors and sale of semen should be made illegal." See *The Sunday Times,* 24 July, 1960.

[284] Address to the Italian Association of Midwives, 29 October, 1951. Compare his Address to the Fourth International Congress of Catholic Doctors, 29 September, 1949: "Artificial insemination outside of marriage is simply and absolutely to be condemned. The natural law and the divine law prescribe that the procreation of a new life may only be the fruit of marriage. It is marriage alone which safeguards the dignity of the partners . . . Artificial insemination in marriage by means of seed derived from a third person is equally immoral and is therefore likewise to be condemned without appeal. Only the marriage partners have mutual rights over one another's body for the procreation of new life; and these rights are exclusive, non-transferable, inalienable. The same

applies if one considers the child. Whoever gives life to an infant has imposed on him by nature, in virtue of this link, the responsibility for the rearing and educating of that infant. But between the lawful spouse and the child who is born of a third person's seed there is no link of parenthood, no moral or juridical link of conjugal procreation." For the relevant texts see R. Kothen, *Directives recentes de l'Église concernant l'exercice de la médecine,* pp. 98-101.

13

Euthanasia

The Reverend Mr. Fletcher entitles his chapter
on this subject: "Euthanasia: Our Right to Die."
His introductory remarks are commendably candid
about the realities which lie behind the pleasant
word "euthanasia." It is, he says, the "deliberate
easing into death of a patient suffering from a painful and fatal disease." He quotes a description of
euthanasia as the "theory that in certain circumstances, when owing to disease, senility or the like,
a person's life has permanently ceased to be either
agreeable or useful, the sufferer should be painlessly
killed, either by himself or by another."[285] The literature of the subject abounds in pity. Phrases like
"merciful release from incurable suffering," "gently
and humanely extinguishing the patient's life," recur on every page. The Reverend Mr. Fletcher,
mindful of his Christian calling, find scriptural war-
rant for "mercy-killing"; doctors who practise it
are, he claims, meriting the beatitude: "Blessed are
the merciful"; they are carrying out the supreme
Christian law of love: "All things whatsoever you
would that men should do unto you, do you even

187

so also unto them."[286] Even Dr. Glanville Williams, who rarely finds himself on the side of Scripture, argues that euthanasia fulfils the greatest of all Christian commandments, that of love.[287] Further examination will show the ambiguities of this reasoning and the horrible traps and snares concealed in it.

Defenders of euthanasia oscillate between attempting to justify it as suicide and attempting to sanction it as blameless or "unselfish" homicide. To justify euthanasia it is obviously necessary to justify suicide; but, as we shall see, it is not sufficient to do so; the case for euthanasia necessarily entails legal and moral approval for some forms of homocide as well. Indeed the real point at issue is the definition of the sanctity of life; and the decision as to whether human life is, as such, inviolable; or whether its inviolability depends on circumstances, on, for example, the "quality," or the social usefulness of the life in question.

Dr. Glanville Williams devotes a chapter to "The Prohibition of Suicide"; he is anxious for reform of the law on suicide in its own right, apart from its connection with the movement for legalization of euthanasia. It is regrettable that he should have confused himself and his chapter with so much bad history, bad moral philosophy and bad theology. His lack of knowledge about these subjects is quite embarrassing. Without them, the chapter would have been much shorter, but far more effective. In fact the Christian will have sympathy with much of the plea for revision or abolition of the criminal law penalties for attempted suicide. A recent student of the subject, writing from a Catholic standpoint, has said: "The man who has hovered over the abyss of self-destruction needs something very different from external penalties: he needs much treatment and he needs great love."[288]

Since, however, Dr. Glanville Williams has dragged so much history, ethics and theology into his argument, it is necessary to make some examination of his views on these aspects of the subject. Most of his information, and most of his errors, on these subjects come from what he calls the "classical" work of Alfred Bayet, *Le suicide et la morale,* published in 1922. Much has been written on the problem of suicide, before, since and about Bayet's work, of which Dr. Glanville Williams has not taken cognisance. It is Bayet who misleads him into confusing suicide with martyrdom and thus into the foolish notion that the early Christian Church approved of suicide.[289]

Bayet's mistake came from his adoption of the definition of suicide given by Durkheim, as "any case of death resulting directly and indirectly from a positive or negative act performed by the victim himself and which he knew would produce this result."[290] This sort of definition was required by Durkheim's sociological preconceptions: definitions of ethical and social phenomena, in order to be "scientific" had to be "objective" and could take no account of "subjective" factors such as motive. Such "objectivism," however, simply ignores the factor in human actions which makes them specifically human and moral. In this context, it has led Durkheim and those who follow him to confuse two actions which are humanly and morally totally different, self-destruction and self-sacrifice.[291] The former is an act of despair and cowardice; the latter an act of hope and faith and courage. The former is egoism and self-love *à outrance;* the latter is highest altruism and the unsurpassable love by which a man lays down his life for his fellow-men. Suicide is the disvaluing of life and of all values; self-sacrifice to the point of death is affirming the reality of values which make life worth living but which are worth more than life.[292] What is missing from Dr. Glanville Williams's discussion of suicide is any understanding of its metaphysical significance and its ultimate moral meaning. He has not seen, with Kant, that

> to annihilate in one's own person the subject of morality is to extirpate from the world, as far as it lies in one, the very existence of morality.[293]

He has not seen, with Chesterton, that

> Not only is suicide a sin, it is the sin. It is the ultimate and absolute evil, the refusal to take an interest in existence; the refusal to take the oath of loyalty to life . . . The man who kills himself, kills all men; as far as he is concerned, he wipes out the world . . . The martyr is noble exactly because . . . he con-

fesses this ultimate link with life; he sets his heart outside himself: he dies that something may live. The suicide is ignoble because he has not this link with being: he is a mere destroyer; spiritually, he destroys the universe.[294]

Suicide is not an individual choice alone but a philosophy of total despair embodied in one desperate act. It is a despair of man and of God; a refusal of effort and of grace; a desertion of time, a denial of eternity. The question of suicide involves a whole philosophy of life.[295] Our attitude to suicide engages our entire scheme of moral values.[296] The public attitude to suicide tests society's evaluation of man as a whole. The suicide rate of a society is a tragic criterion of the validity of its whole way of life. Suicide is universally agreed to be a phenomenon of failure of social and individual integration.[297] Suicide occurs when society has failed to give a man faith in his fellow-men, and his personal beliefs have ceased to give him reasons for hoping against human hope, or for faith in God who will not fail. If the decline of Christian belief and of Christian morals continues, as Dr. Glanville Williams anticipates—and strives—that it shall, we can hardly but expect that the incidence of and the social indifference to suicide will increase.[298] This is why it is so much to be deplored that his admirable plea for sympathy for the suicide should be accompanied by a defence of the moral rightness of suicide and an attack on the Christian philosophy of life. It is to the consequences of abandoning the Christian doctrine of the sanctity of life that we now turn.

Dr. Glanville Williams ends his chapter on suicide with this paragraph:

On the whole, then, it is submitted that the law might well exempt from punishment the unsefish abetment of suicide and the unselfish homicide upon request. This rule would solve at a stroke the problem of voluntary euthanasia in cases of fatal illness. It would, of course, go much beyond the legal change usually advocated by supporters of euthanasia, because it would not be limited to persons suffering from an incurable and painful illness. Since it is probably too radical a change in the law for present public opinion in the English-speaking countries, more limited proposals for the legalization of euthanasia will be canvassed in the next chapter.[299]

The "limited proposals" are that "all suffering patients in fatal illnesses may have voluntary euthanasia."[300] But we shall see constantly throughout the argument, and we are explicitly told by Dr. Glanville Williams again at the end, that this is no logical stopping place. The obstacle, of course, is Christian teaching;[301] both because of its absolute prohibition of any deliberate taking of life; and because, it is alleged, of its masochistic and fatalistic view that suffering is God's will for us and is inherently good and that it is wrong to interfere with the course of nature in order to avoid or lessen pain.

The ancient opinion that religion requires resignation and that the more unpleasant of two alternatives has some intrinsic moral superiority, has lost nearly all its support.[302]

Let us simply juxtapose with this some sentences from the late Pope Pius XII's allocution to the Italian Society for the Science of Anaesthetics in February, 1957, on Religious and Moral Aspects of Pain Prevention in Medical Practice:

In the first place, you ask whether there is a general moral obligation to endure physical pain . . . It is evident that in certain cases the acceptance of physical suffering is a matter of serious obligation. Thus a man is bound in conscience to accept suffering whenever he is faced with the inescapable alternative of enduring suffering or of acting contrary to a moral obligation, either by positive action or by omission. Man, even after the Fall, retains the right of control over the forces of Nature, of employing them for his own use, and consequently of deriving benefit from all the resources which it offers him either to suppress or to avoid physical pain . . .[303] The Christian is bound to mortify his flesh and to strive after his interior purification, for it is impossible, in the long run, to avoid sin and to carry out all one's duties faithfully, if this effort at

mortification and purification be neglected.
Physical suffering becomes a necessity and
must be accepted to the extent that, without
its aid, mastery over self and disorderly tendencies is unattainable; but in so far as it is not
required for this purpose, one cannot assert
that there exists a strict obligation in the matter. The Christian, then, is never obliged to
will suffering for its own sake; he considers it
according to circumstances, as a means more
or less suited to the end which he is pursuing . . . The acceptance of suffering is only
one way, among many others, of indicating
what is the real essential: the will to love
God and to serve Him in all things. It is,
above all, in the perfection of this voluntary
disposition that the quality of the Christian
life and its heroism consists.[304]

In the same address, the Pope dealt expressly
with the questions of euthanasia and of the use of
pain-killing drugs which have the effect of shortening life. Dr. Glanville Williams claims familiarity
with these texts and indeed is pleased to think that,
in them, the Pope took an important step towards
enlightened contemporary opinion. He suggests that,
in fact, the Pope was "redefining the time of death"
and distinguishing between mere vegetable life and
genuinely human life. This leaves him not without
hope that some day the Church may apply this logic
to the other end of the life-scale and redefine the
time of beginning of human life, thus allowing the

embryo to be disposed of as the mere vegetable organism which it is.[305] It is a pity that he is so ill-informed about the nature of Catholic teaching that he thinks that Popes invent it at need and change it according to circumstance. But it is important to be clear about what the Pope did say in restating the traditional Catholic teaching about these questions; and Pope Pius XII's words, as always, were clear enough to be easily understood and to need no exegesis. We quote from him:

> We have now to examine your third question: "Is it permitted . . . to use analgesic treatments . . . even in the case of the dying and of patients in danger of death, when there is a medical reason for their use? Is this permitted even in certain cases (inoperable cancers and incurable diseases) where the lessening of the unbearable pain is achieved probably at the cost of the duration of life, which is thereby shortened?" . . . To declare that the dying have a greater moral obligation than others—whether from Natural Law or from Christian teaching—to accept suffering, is in keeping neither with the nature of things nor with the sources of Revelation.[306] The use of anaesthetics at the approach of death with the sole purpose of depriving the sick person of consciousness at the end would not be a notable gain in the art of modern healing, but a practice truly to be regretted. Your question was proposed

rather on the supposition that a serious medical reason existed (e.g., violent pains, path-
ological states of depression and agony) . . .
Would it be necessary to give up (the use of
drugs) if the actual effect . . . was to shorten
the span of life? First, all forms of direct
euthanasia, i.e., the administration of a drug
in order to produce or hasten death, is un-
lawful because in that case a claim is being
made to dispose directly of life . . . If there
exists no direct causal link, either through
the will of interested parties or by the nature
of things, between the induced unconscious-
ness and the shortening of life—as would be
the case if the suppression of pain could be
obtained only by the shortening of life; and
if, on the other hand, the actual administration of drugs brings about two distinct effects, the one the relief of pain, the other
the shortening of life, the action is lawful.[307]

Dr. Glanville Williams here, as elsewhere, tries
to discredit the "doctrine of double effect."[308] But
without this doctrine, no morality could stand. As
he himself remarks: "there is no human conduct
from which evil cannot be imagined to follow";[309]
hence the distinction between morally good and
morally bad human conduct turns on the distinction
between conduct which has some evil thing for its
intended and directly produced effect, on the one
hand; and, on the other, conduct which directly
produces and intends a good effect, though evil con-

sequences may be foreseen as likely or even inevitable, through uncontrollable circumstances or the evil use men choose to make of lawful pursuits and good inventions. Research physicists, and indeed scientists of all varieties, engineers, inventors, lawyers, educationists, publicans—all of whose services and products are abused by wicked or misguided men—are living by the double effect doctrine all the time.[310]

In the present context, Dr. Glanville Williams knows very well that the double effect doctrine of Catholic moralists, so far from favouring his proposals for legal and moral permission for euthanasia, is the immovable obstacle in their path. He knows very well that and all the dust he raises cannot obscure, the distinction between setting out to kill a patient, and setting out to relieve a patient's pain. There is a difference of nature and not just of motive between choosing a dose of narcotic which is calculated to be enough to kill, and a dose which is regulated by the need to make pain bearable.[311] It would be waste of time to argue about the difference. It is all the difference between Dr. Glanville Williams and Christianity. It is what his whole book is about.

We have already argued in Chapter Seven that Dr. Glanville William's views in fact constitute a whole philosophy of man according to which human life is not *as such* sacred or inviolable. Whether life is sacred or not is made to depend upon its "quality" and "usefulness."[312] This is the inevitable consequence of a certain kind of scientific human-ism. Seeking to explain man exclusively in natural-science terms, it comes to speak of man as of a scientific object. From this, it is fatally easy to get used to adopting towards men the attitudes, plans and policies appropriate to things. Professor J. Z. Young wishes to substitute "tool language" for "person-language" in order to understand and de-scribe man scientifically.[312a] For limited purposes, this is useful. But who can fail to see the danger of forgetting that man is a person, of coming to think of man *as such* as a tool? When tools are obsolete, we replace them; when they are useless, we scrap or smelt them. Euthanasia is a link in that logic: when men are useless, we kill them; only "gently and humanely," for they are "animated tools."[313]

There could be few graver threats to morality and civilization than that presented by the ideology of euthanasia. More than half a century ago the man who gave us the word "agnostic," Thomas Henry Huxley, wrote:

> I sometimes wonder whether people, who talk so freely about extirpating the unfit, ever dispassionately consider their own his-tory. Surely one must be very "fit," indeed, not to know of an occasion, or perhaps two, in one's life, when it would have been only too easy to qualify for a place among the "unfit."[314]

Let us look further into the logic of euthanasia and the meaning of "unfit" in the dictionary of euthanasia-advocates. We saw that the proposals for voluntary euthanasia are limited and tentative. They must be regarded as only a first installment. A law legalizing voluntary euthanasia would, in itself, have an inescapable vagueness which would make its interpretation and control extremely difficult. There are obvious difficulties of diagnosis and prognosis: how often can doctors be *certain* that the illness is fatal or death imminent? If euthanasia mentality were to spread among doctors—and relatives—it would surely be somewhat naive to share Dr. Glanville Williams's confidence that doctors will seldom err.[315] Their errors would then be so irreparable. A lawyer, with experience of last wills and testaments made *in extremis,* should be more aware than most of the difficulties of determining the presence of "consent," "sound mind," the absence of "undue influence," such as would be required to give a valid and irrevocable consent to one's own killing, in the last stages of a painful illness. The circumstances for which voluntary euthanasia is envisaged are, in fact, such as would make *voluntary* euthanasia a legal fiction.[316]

There are, of course, illnesses which do not impair capacity for rational deliberation. If "voluntary" euthanasia be permitted in fatal illnesses where the voluntariness of the demand for it is doubtful, can it be refused in less grave cases where that voluntariness is certain? Dr. Glanville Williams says it cannot:

The question of legalizing suicide and voluntary euthanasia in specific circumstances does not confine itself to the case of the painful, fatal illness. There is, for example, the incapacitating but non-painful affliction, such as paralysis. Has a man the right to demand to be released from a living death, if he regards his affliction as that? . . . Again a person who knows himself to have contracted a mortal disease may, even in its early stages, wish for euthanasia in order to save himself from total dependence on others.[317]

Strange and terrible is the logic of euthanasia. Its advocates begin by carefully insisting that euthanasia is propsed only for suffering patients in the last stages of fatal illnesses, but soon they are explaining that the patient need not be suffering, death need not be imminent, the illness need not be fatal, for euthanasia to be reasonable and defensible. They begin by piously protesting that euthanasia is proposed only for those who voluntarily request it; but soon they are observing that some people who would be much better dead are incapable of asking to be put to death. Can euthanasia be logically refused them just because they cannot voluntarily request it? Dr. Glanville Williams shows us how the logic works:

If the present attitude towards suicide were reversed, the problems of voluntary euthanasia, where an exercise of volition is possible, would be largely solved. But the argument for a change in attitude becomes far less strong when the attention is turned to involuntary euthanasia, as for example in the case of senile dementia. It may, indeed, be that mankind will one day have to revise its present ethics of keeping people alive. It is increasingly common for men and women to reach an age of "second childishness and mere oblivion" with a loss of almost all adult faculties except that of digestion . . . These facts are reflected in increasing rates of admission to mental hospitals, increasing numbers in those hospitals, and constant problems of overcrowding . . . Only the grimmest necessity could bring about a change that, however cautious in its approach, would probably cause apprehension and deep distress to many people, and inflict a traumatic injury upon the accepted code of behaviour built up by two thousand years of the Christian religion. It may be, however, that as the problem becomes more acute, it will itself cause a reversal of generally accepted values.[318] . . . The other problem of involuntary euthanasia is in respect of hopelessly defective infants. While the Euthanasia Society of England has never advocated this, the Euthanasia Society of America did include it in its original programme. The proposal certainly escapes the chief objection to the similar proposal for senile dementia: it does not create a sense of insecurity in society, because infants cannot, like adults, feel anticipatory dread of being done to death if their condition should worsen. Moreover, the proposal receives some support on humanitarian grounds both on account of the parents, to whom the child will be a burden all their lives, and on account of the handicapped child itself. (It is not, however, proposed that any child should be destroyed against the wishes of its parents.) Finally, the legalization of euthanasia for handicapped children would bring the law into closer relation to its practical administration, because juries do not regard parental mercy-killing as murder. For these various reasons the proposal to legalize humanitarian infanticide is put forward from time to time by individuals. They remain in a very small minority and the proposal may at present be dismissed as politically significant. However . . . even the present law which forbids humanitarian infanticide is capable of being interpreted or applied in a merciful manner.[319]

And so ends *The Sanctity of Life and the Criminal Law*. We have stressed, and we repeat, that the end is contained in the beginning. To approve of Dr. Glanville Williams's *principles* in the case of e.g. contraception, is to leave oneself with no *reason* for moral condemnation of the killing of sickly or deformed or defective infants, mental defectives, the incurably sick, the senile. There is an inexorable logic connecting contraception, through abortion, sterilization and eugenic parenthood, with the (painless) elimination of the "unfit" or the "socially inadequate."[320]

This logic does not lie only in the future. It has been the official policy of a powerful and scientifically advanced nation in our time. The Nazis had the iron will to "revise our present ethics of keeping people alive." An implacable logic led from the sterilization laws of 1933 to Buchenwald. Professor Leibbrand, Professor of Medical History at the Erlangen Faculty, and witness for the prosecution at the Nuremberg trial of Nazi doctors, traced the beginning of the medical horrors of Nazi Germany to the substitution of the "biological idea" for the "metaphysical idea," which was present already in the sterilization laws of 1933.[321] It is the explicit demand of Dr. Glanville Williams and his friends that we should substitute biological for metaphysical concepts in our attitudes towards and laws concerning sex and procreation, birth and death. This is, indeed, the demand of a great deal of modern philosophy and ethics, the slogan of much contemporary scientific humanism and agnostic liberalism.[322] Many defenders of these ideas are humane, warm-hearted men, dedicated to the improvement of humanity. So were some of those tried at Nuremberg.[323] It is earnestly to be hoped that liberals and humanists, who abominate Nazism as much as we do, will abandon a road that can only lead to new Buchenwalds.

Let us, meanwhile, give the last word on euthanasia to the Nazis, who have first right to it.

When it was discovered that the use of anti-gangrenous serum employed by the Army Health Service had caused many accidents when applied to the wounded, Mrugowski Chief of the S.S. Hygenic Service), suspecting the phenol contained in the serum, ordered Dr. Ding to attend some sessions of euthanasia with phenol in a concentration camp, and to send him a detailed account of the results, because he had never seen a death caused by phenol. "Some days later," reported Dr. Ding at the trial of doctors, "I asked Howen of Buchenwald to advise me about the next session of euthanasia with phenol. The following evening, he called me to the hospital . . . The injection consisted of 20 cubic cm. of raw, undiluted phenol. One by one, the four or five prisoners were introduced . . . They were advanced in years and poor in health. I do not remember the reason why euthanasia was practised, but I probably did not ask the reason. The prisoners sat quietly on a chair beside a lamp, and showed no emotion. A male nurse blocked the vein of the arm and Dr. Howen injected the phenol quickly. They died during the injection, without any signs of pain and in less than a second. I remained there about ten minutes. In accordance with the orders I had received, I made my report to Berlin."[324]

[285] P. 172. Dr. Glanville Williams is inspired to near-poetry by this subject: he speaks of the sufferer's right "to pass upon the midnight without pain" (p. 306).

[286] Pp. 183, 195, 197.

[287] P. 282.

[288] L. Meynard, *Le suicide,* Etude morale et métaphysique, Presses Universitaires de France, 1958, p. 9.

[289] Pp. 229-231. Lecky (1911) remains, of course, a primary source on Christian history for Dr. Glanville Williams, and has been liberally drawn on here. The Circumcelliones are somehow taken as typifying the early Church. St. Augustine felt that the suicide-martyr business had got to be stopped: so he pioneered the doctrine that suicide is evil! Paul-Louis Landsberg, in *The Moral Problem of Suicide,* E. trans. Rockliff, London, 1953, pp. 73-8, criticises Bayet's definition of suicide and completely rejects the allegation that the Christian martyrs were suicides. Dr. Glanville Williams (pp. 241-3) quotes Landsberg; but he either did not take time to read, or was not interested in, the critique of Bayet, which is an important part of Landsberg's short essay.

[290] E. Durkheim, *Le suicide,* Alcan, Paris, 1897, p. 5. Despite his misleading definition, Durkheim did not make Bayet's mistake of thinking that the early Church approved of suicide. He, in fact, traces back to early Christian teaching the absolute moral condemnation of suicide characteristic of European civilization (pp. 370 ff.).

[291] Halbwachs, writing as a sociologist, saw the error of Durkheim's definition and substituted the following: "Suicide is any case of death resulting from an act accomplished by the victim, with the intention or foreseen result of killing himself, and which is not an act of self-sacrifice." (In *Les causes du suicide,* Paris, 1930, cited by L. Meynard in op. cit., p. 60.) Landsberg's definition (op. cit., p. 76) is: "Suicide is the act by which a human being deliberately creates

what he considers to be an effective and adequate cause of his own death."

292 Compare Landsberg, loc. cit., and p. 95. No testimony on the question of suicide could be more impressive than that of Paul-Louis Landsberg, the Jewish philosopher and refugee from Nazism. He struggled with it as a personal temptation and problem for much of his life. For many years he carried poison on his person, determined to use it in order to win "liberty" by self-chosen death should he be arrested by the Nazis. He grew, however, through suffering, in spiritual maturity and came closer and closer to the Catholic faith. When he eventually fell into the hands of the Gestapo in 1943, he had already destroyed the poison and he accepted imprisonment, torture and eventual death (at Oranienburg in 1944) without abandoning "determination, goodness, faith." It is this which gives such depth and power to his essays on death and on suicide. Compare J. M. Osterreicher, *Walls are Crumbling,* Hollis and Carter, London, 1953, pp. 225-231. Landsberg's journey from suicide was a journey to Christ. Just before his arrest, he wrote: "I have now met Christ." We may recall Barbey d'Aurevilly's words to Baudelaire after reading the *Fleurs du Mal:* "You have no alternative but to blow your brains out or to become a Christian." A very valuable discussion of the morality of suicide and of its difference from sacrifice, martyrdom and asceticism is to be found in René le Senne's *Traité de Morale Générale,* Presses Univ. de France, 1949, pp. 484-6, 655-8. (He observes that the notions of martyrdom and sacrifice of life and self-denial are an insoluble paradox for utilitarianism.) Compare L. Meynard, op. cit., pp. 24 ff., 57 ff.; Max Scheler, *Le sens de la souffrance,* French trans., Aubier, Paris, 1936, pp. 9-21; Georges Gargan, *L'amour et la mort,* Edits du Seuil, Paris, 1959, esp. pp. 91-143, 281 ff.

293 From *Tugendlehere,* cited in *Dictionnaire de Théologie Catholique,* s.v. Suicide, t. XIV-2, col. 2746.

294 *Orthodoxy,* John Lane, 1943 ed., pp. 115-7. Compare L. Meynard, op. cit., pp. 64, 76-9, 86.

295 Compare Camille Schuwer, *La signification métaphysique du suicide,* Aubier, Paris, 1949, pp. 25-6; Gabriel Deshaies, *Psychologie du suicide,* Presses Univ. de France, 1947, pp. 39, 146-151, 324 ff. Both of these, and particularly

Schuwer, make valuable points; but both are led into a sophistical exculpation of suicide, largely through the influence of the errors of Bayet. Bayet had argued that, though suicide may be wrong for the uncultured masses, by the standards of ordinary morality, it may be good and right for "cultivated élites" in the light of their superior morality. (See Le Senne, op. cit., pp. 484-5.) Similarly Schuwer argues that the suicide places himself outside morality and therefore cannot be judged by moral standards at all (op. cit., pp. 103, 145-6, 160-1). The point surely is whether it is morally right—or possible—to "place oneself outside morality"; and surely one of the agreed propositions among moralists is that one may not exempt oneself from general moral rules, or make oneself a moral exception. To do so might indeed be taken as a definition of immorality. Deshaies falls into the less sophisticated error, again after Bayet, of confusing suicide with martyrdome: his argument is that suicide is morally right because a St. Thomas More is morally admirable! (opp. cit., pp. 226-234).

296 This is a favourite theme of Gabriel Marcel. See, e.g., *Position et Approches concrètes du mystère ontologique,* Nauwelaerts, Louvain, 1949, pp. 66-7: "The permanent possibility of suicide is . . . perhaps the essential starting point in all genuine metaphysical thinking." From the possibility of total despair Marcel goes on to discern the existence in man of a reality which is not to be satisfied by all worldly "having," which aspires beyond all empirical achievements; and in this he finds grounds for a hope in Transcendent Being beyond all empirical verifications. Camus may be said to have been at the beginning of this itinerary when he began *Le Mythe de Sisyphe* (Gallimard, Paris, 1942) by declaring: "There is only one really serious philosophical problem, and that is suicide. To decide whether life is or is not worth living is to answer the fundamental question of philosophy."

297 See Durkheim, op. cit., pp. 215-232. He found divorce and suicide to vary in direct proportion, and held that this was precisely because divorce introduces instability into family life and instability and insecurity are as such suicidogenic: "the very institution of divorce, by the action it exerts within marriage, predisposes towards suicide." See op. cit.,

pp. 289-311; compare pp. 424-442. Compare Deshaies, op. cit., pp. 30-6.

[298] There is a significant negative correlation, noted by all observers, between religious belief and suicide rate. Catholics are notably less prone to suicide than Protestants (Jews are less prone than either). See tables and analyses in Durkheim, pp. 149-170; Deshaies, pp. 39-43. Durkheim seeks to explain this correlation by saying that religion affects suicide-rates, not because of its doctrine, but because it provides the individual with social solidarity and cohesion (—and forbids him to think!). Catholicism is more anti-suicidogenic because its social structure is tighter and firmer (—and its prohibition of thought more effective!) (op. cit., pp. 160-170, 430-2). Durkheim's anxiety was: Christianity is on the way out anyhow (since this almost the twentieth century!); how, then, can society defend itself against suicide without the help of religious myths? He tries to find in the objective reality and needs of society a ground for the unqualified moral condemnation of suicide. Then he looks to social reform and social security to provide the psychological defences against suicide (pp. 428-442). His hopes are scarcely borne out by contemporary experience. Sweden's high suicide rate is not to be explained through the lack of either material prosperity or social security. Ireland's suicide rate is the lowest in the world. The latest figures released by W.H.O. show that, per 100,000 population, Ireland has 4.4 suicides; Denmark 30.2; Sweden 31.2; Switzerland 31.9; Austria 32.4; Finland 37.0; West Berlin 43.2. See daily press, 15 March, 1960.

[299] Op. cit., p. 276.

[300] P. 281. In a broadcast discussion on the B.B.C., on 22 January, 1959, he said that euthanasia must be voluntary; compulsory euthanasia would be "disastrous."

[301] "If it is true," he writes, "that euthanasia can be condemned only according to a religious opinion, this should be sufficient at the present day to remove the prohibition from the criminal law" (p. 278).

[302] P. 278; compare p. 280. On p. 241 there is a very regrettable sentence, written perhaps facetiously to raise audience-laughs: "May not even the most sadistic God be satisfied if he has succeeded in driving a man to suicide." It is written

in a reference to Paul-Louis Landsberg, who was broken by Nazi sadism, and gave his soul with thanks to God, at Oranienburg. Lest we forget the Reverend Mr. Fletcher, he is still with us, prattling away against the "ethical inertia," "pure vitalism," "fatalism" of the traditional Christian view (pp. 185, 186-7, 196-7).

[303] The Holy Father said this after recalling his address of 8 January, 1956, on Painless Childbirth: "There it was asked whether, by virtue of the text in Scripture, 'In sorrow shalt thou bring forth children' (Gen. iii, 16), the mother was obliged to accept all the sufferings and to refuse relief from pain by either natural or artificial means. We answered that there was no obligation of this kind."

[304] Translation published by the Catholic Truth Society of Ireland, pp. 9-11.

[305] This was the burthen of one of his arguments in a B.B.C. broadcast discussion with Miss G. E. M. Anscombe, Professor Max Gluckman and Professor W. C. W. Nixon, on 22 January, 1959. We have called attention in Chapter Ten to the logical and moral equivalence of abortion and euthanasia and to the significant recognition of this by scientific humanists.

[306] The Pope went on to speak further about the spiritual role of suffering; the words recall what he had earlier said about suffering in the Christian life, but they should be quoted for their own sake (and remembering Dr. Glanville Williams's taunts of Christian masochism): "The growth in the love of God and in abandonment to His will does not come from the sufferings themselves which are accepted, but from the intention in the will supported by grace. This intention, in many of the dying, can be strengthened and become more active if their sufferings are eased, for these sufferings increase the state of weakness and physical exhaustion, check the ardour of the soul and sap the moral powers instead of sustaining them. On the other hand, the suppression of pain removes any tension in body and mind, renders prayer easy, and makes possible a more generous gift of self. If some dying persons accept their suffering as a means of expiation and a source of merits . . . do not force anaesthetics on them . . . Where the situation is entirely different, it would be inadvisable to suggest to dying persons the ascetical consid-

erations set out above; and it is to be remembered that instead of assisting towards expiation and merit, suffering can also furnish occasion for new faults" (op. cit., pp. 20-1).

307 Op. cit., pp. 19-23.

308 Compare p. 99 (re sterilization); pp. 183-4 (re therapeutic abortion).

309 P. 281.

310 Dr. Glanville Williams says (p. 286): "When a result is foreseen as certain, it is the same as if it were desired or intended. It would be an undue refinement to distinguish between the two." If this be true, then, to trace the causal lines no further, Marconi was responsible for Goebbels, Wilbur and Orville Wright for the bombing of Coventry and Dresden, Lord Rutherford for the horrors of Hiroshima.

311 We leave it to reasonable men to judge this sentence: "It is altogether too artificial to say that a doctor who gives an *overdose* of a narcotic having *in the forefront of his mind the aim of ending his patient's existence* is guilty of sin; while a doctor who gives the same overdose in the same circumstances *in order to relieve pain* is not guilty of sin, provided that he keeps his mind steadily off the consequence which his professional training teaches him is inevitable, namely the death of his patient" (p. 286, italics ours). It is surely disingenuous to pretend that intentions, aims and attitudes do not morally matter. But the two situations do not differ only in intention and attitude of mind. The difference between them is blurred by the repetition of the word *overdose;* but the word is equivocal. An *overdose* is defined by its relation to the purpose of the dose, so that the purpose determines the nature of the act; and the purpose is admittedly different in the two cases. It is unjust to try to suggest that the second doctor is being merely hypocritical in "keeping his mind steadily off" the consequence of his patient's death. The doctrine of double effect is not a doctrine of doublethink. It does not require a man to pretend not to foresee what he does foresee. It requires him not to *desire* an evil thing as an end and as a means; not to *intend* evil or to *bring about* evil in order that good may come. And that is nearly all of morals.

312 See pp. 52-4 above, with the quotations from Dr. Glanville Williams and the Reverend Mr. Fletcher there given.

Let us simply recall one sentence from the former: "It is good that men should feel a horror of taking human life, but in a rational judgment the quality of the life must be considered" (p. 281; cf. p. 299).

312a In a lecture at Queen's University, Belfast, in November, 1954; compare his B.B.C. Reith Lectures, published as *Doubt and Certainty in Science,* Oxford, 1951, especially pp. 14-23.

313 This is, of course, Aristotle's celebrated definition of a slave. We have quoted passages from Dr. Glanville Williams (see pp. 12-13 above) which seem to "assume that what is right treatment for animals is, *eo ipso,* right treatment for men." Here again, it is part of his propaganda for euthanasia to suggest that just as it is wrong not to put a suffering animal out of pain, so it is wrong not to put a suffering human being out of pain. See p. 293. The Reverend Mr. Fletcher, with his usual artlessness, writes: "It seems unimaginable that either Schweitzer or Gandhi would deny to a human being what they would render with however heavy a heart, to a calf" (p. 193; on euthanasia for dogs, see p. 204).

314 In the Prolegomena to his Romanes lecture, 1893, published along with his grandson Julian's Romanes lecture of exactly 50 years later, in *Evolution and Ethics,* Pilot Press, London, 1947 (the reference is to p. 56). The elder Huxley's lecture on "Evolution and Ethics" had as a dominant theme the argument that the morality stands opposed to the "gladiatorial theory of existence" embodied in the Darwinian notion of natural selection and the survival of the fittest, which, of course, he accepted as the explanation of man's origin. Contrast Dr. Glanville Williams, p. 83: "We have evolved by natural selection, but, by keeping alive mentally and physically ill-equipped children, we are opposing natural selection." There is, of course, a good of philosophy written about ethics and evolution; and Dr. Glanville Williams does not seem familiar with it.

315 See pp. 301-2 and cf. p. 154. He assures us that many doctors are anticipating the law and practising euthanasia already; the law should therefore, he declares, be brought into accord with their practice (p. 304).

316 Dr. Glanville Williams recognizes this difficulty (pp.

306-8) but concludes: "Every law has to face some difficulties in application, and these difficulties are not a conclusive argument against a law if it has a beneficial operation" (p 307).

317 P. 309.

318 Pp. 309-310.

319 Pp. 311-312. Professor Portes, of the French Academy of Medicine, in the Cahiers Laennec studies on Euthanasia, translated and published in *New Problems in Medical Ethics,* III, ed. by Dom Peter Flood, Mercier Press, Cork, 1956, pp. 261-299, writes: "If the doctor can establish an infallible prognosis of incurability in a given case, why limit the beneficent action of euthanasia to patients who are conscious of their agony? Why not extend it to the incurable patient who is unconscious? To the paralytic who is a burden to his family? To the idiot who is a burden on the rates? To the mentally defective and the degenerate who figure so largely among delinquents? . . . To the deaf and dumb and to the blind when no institution has enabled them to adapt themselves to social life? etc. . . ." (op. cit., p. 274; compare pp. 262, 289-290, 298). We pointed out (see pp. 85-6) that the Reverend Mr. Fletcher uses words which—if he understood them—mean that he approves of euthanasia for anyone who is deranged or chronically unconscious: "A patient who has completely lost the power to communicate has passed into a subnormal state . . . Being no longer responsive, he is no longer responsible" (p. 201).

320 Compare *New Problems in Medical Ethics, III*, pp. 289-290.

321 Quoted by Father Gonzague Pierre in "Experimentation in Nazi Germany from 1940-1945," one of the Cahiers Laennec studies, *L'experimentation humanie en médecine,* Lethielleux, Paris, 1952. This has been translated as *Medical Experimentation on Man,* ed. by Dom Peter Flood, Mercier Press, Cork, 1955. References are to the English edition. The present reference is to p. 133.

322 On its influence in medical thinking, compare Remy Collin, *Plaidoyers pour la vie humaine,* La Colombe, Paris, 1952, pp. 218-245; René Biot, *Santé Humaine and Offensives biologiques contre la personne,* passim.

323 Mitscherlich and Milke, in their study of the Nuremberg

trials, say of the incriminated doctors: "Until the war and the dictatorship created the situations we know of, these men were irreproachable citizens, happy in their researches or in their professional medical activity. The fact that they did not resist the suggestions made to them can be ascribed to human weakness; but it may be ascribed equally to the character of their ideas and to the habits they had derived from their scientific education itself . . ."; and they go on to speak of the danger of a dehumanization of medicine through the ideology of scientific nautralism. (*Medical Eperimentation on Man,* pp. 141-4). The case of Professor Schilling, retired Director of the Tropical Diseases Section of the Robert Koch Institute, who was 71 when he began his barbarous experiments at Dachau, is particularly disconcerting (op. cit., pp. 130-2). A reviewer (in the *Sunday Times,* 28 June, 1959) of the recent autobiography of Rudolf Hoess, *Commandant of Auschwitz,* writes: "His character was marked by all these qualities which we are rightly most called upon to admire: iron determination, energy, selflessness, obedience and devotion to duty. He dearly loved his wife and children, knew compassion for his fellow human beings and . . . ever regarded a good book as a good friend."

324 *Medical Experimentation on Man,* pp. 123-4. One of the most ghastly of Nazi crimes was the causing of most horrible deaths to some sixty persons in experiments designed to determine the perfect dosage of cyanide of potassium for the eventual suicide of the great Nazi chiefs (op. cit., pp. 125-6). What a commentary on Bayet's "morale nuancée" of the "élites cultivées"!

14

The Way
Back to Sanity

The ethics of scientific humanism begins by recognizing only one moral principle, the law of humanitarian compassion, the law of pity; it ends by justifying the putting to death of those who have always been, in civilized societies, the natural objects of compassion and pity. If the objects of pity are to be eliminated on humanist principles, then, by these same principles, must not pity itself perish from the earth? The language of many humanists envisages a world where there is no longer any need for pity. Dr. Glanville Williams, in a footnote on the last page of his book, quotes Millard S. Everett as saying, in his *Ideals of Life*.[325]

My personal feeling . . . is that eventually, when public opinion is prepared for it, no child shall be admitted into the society of the living who would be certain to suffer any social handicap—for example, any physical or mental defect that would prevent mar-

215

riage or would make others tolerate his company only from a sense of mercy . . .[326]

It is a striking fact that pity, divorced from moral absolutes, ends by destroying itself and turns into inhumanity. Pity for mothers leads to approval of "parental mercy-killing" of deformed or defective children;[327] pity for doctors leads to pleas for releasing them from the legal prohibition of killing patients;[328] pity for relatives leads to proposals for removing, by lethal injection, the burden of dependent invalids and simpletons and senile grandparents or parents.[329] Pity for those who cannot bear the sight of suffering leads to the "humane overdose[330] for the sufferers. Pity for those who have lost the sense of pity leads to death for those who most need pity.

Now it is not the intentions or the sentiments of the humanists which are wrong; Dr. Glanville Williams and his admirers are obviously men of the most humane intentions and the most compassionate sentiments. Rather, it is their thinking which is wrong. They do not seem to have thought their philosophy through to its conclusions or back to its root principles. Their error is metaphysical: a mistake about the nature of man and the meaning of his life on the earth.

Nowhere is this more clearly shown than in their attitude to suffering. Suffering they see as *the* evil; and the abolition of it as *the* good which calls for and justifies even means traditionally regarded as immoral. They do not seem to recognize that suffering can be a means of moral and spiritual growth, that it is the school of great writers, artists, thinkers, saints; that it marks the difference between the deep and the superficial in human understanding. They do not see that suffering, at least the suffering of self-denial and sacrifice, is a condition of all moral living. They do not admit that suffering is part of man's meaning and is necessary both to remind us that we are men and to make us wise men and good men.[331] When men fear suffering more than they fear sin then will justice and fortitude and love and the pursuit of truth perish among men. When men fear sickness in the body more than they fear sickness in the soul, then will it be again, as it was before the Gospel of Christ, that men will be "without affection, without fidelity, without mercy."[332]

Where shall we find the way back to sanity? Unexpectedly, Bertrand Russell helps us to find it. Philip Toynbee, reviewing Russell's *Why I Am Not A Christian*[333] in the *Observer,* on 6 October, 1957, said:

> It is in the moral argument that Russell is weakest. In one appalling passage he shows how the strictly logical mind can, if the eyes are fixed too firmly on the argument and too seldom on the given and visible world, lead us straight to hell:
> "Assuming the break-up of the family and the establishment of rationally-conducted State institutions for children, it will prob-

ably be necessary to go a step further in the regulation of instinct. Women accustomed to birth control and not allowed to keep their own children would have little motive for enduring the discomfort of gestation and the pain of childbirth. Consequently, in order to keep up the population it would probably be necessary to make child-bearing a well-paid profession not, of course, to be undertaken by all women or even by a majority but by a certain percentage who would have to pass tests as to their fitness from a stock-breeding point of view. What tests should be imposed upon sires . . . is a question we are not yet called upon to decide."[334]

The following Sunday, Russell wrote to the *Observer*:

Mr. Toynbee . . . does not realise (though for this the fault is mine) that the passage horrifies me as much as it does him. I was engaged, not in advocacy but in prophecy in the style of Cassandra, but I am to blame for having failed to make this clear.[335] What Mr. Toynbee says in criticism of my views on ethics has my entire sympathy. I find my own views argumentively irrefutable but nevertheless incredible. I do not know the solution.[336]

There is nothing wrong with Lord Russell's powers of logical reasoning. If he arrives at an "appalling" and "incredible" conclusion, this can only be because his premises were false. We could, however, suggest to Lord Russell the solution which is indicated by his own most recent moral thinking. In his eighty-ninth year, Russell is campaigning with astonishing vigour and with a noble passion for nuclear disarmament. In January, 1959, in his little book *Common Sense and Nuclear Warfare*,[337] he said:

> There is no conclusion possible in this march towards insane death except to turn right round and march instead towards sanity and life. Our present courses lead inevitably, sooner or later, to the extinction of the human species. We are not doomed to persist in the race towards disaster. Human volitions have caused it, and human volitions can arrest it.[338]

Now Russell, in *The Scientific Outlook,* showed that the application of "scientific attitudes" to sex and reproduction will lead inevitably to a brutalizing of the human species; and as we have seen, this horrifies him just much as does the prospect of nuclear destruction. What he has not admitted is that his own sexual ethics leads inevitably to the horrors of "scientific reproduction." This, however, is the lesson borne in upon us by our study of his own *Marriage and Morals,* as well as by our study of Dr. Glanville Williams and the Reverend Mr. Fletcher. This has shown that contraception, abortion, sterilization, artificial insemination are as fatal to humanity as are nuclear bombs. Is there any conclusion possible except, in Russell's own words, "to turn right round (from them) and march instead towards sanity and life?" Russell has shown us where the danger lies both in the sphere of sex and in the nuclear arms race; it lies in "power without wisdom"; where wisdom means "a right conception of the ends of life.[339]. Russell has even indicated where the veto to evil power may be found: in Christian ethics.[340] The only way back to sanity and life is a return to Christian faith and love and to Christian respect for the sacredness of sex and marriage and for the absolute sanctity of human life.

[325] New York, 1954.

[326] "Life in early infancy," he goes on, "is very close to non-existence, and admitting a child into our society is almost like admitting one from potential to actual existence, and viewed in this way, only normal life should be accepted." The Reverend Mr. Fletcher speaks of the child's "divine right to be born in freedom from disease and defect" (p. 143). He quotes the White House Conference on Child Health and Protection, 1930, as declaring: "There should be no child in America that has not the complete *birthright* of a sound mind in a sound body, and that has not been born under proper conditions" (p. 141). J. B. S. Haldane (op. cit., p. 102) quotes Miss Peterkin, "a firm American believer in eugenics," as saying: "I do not believe that the care and pity given by the strong to the weak have helped civilization."

[327] Compare Dr. Glanville Williams, p. 321; cf. pp. 31, 293.

[328] Compare Dr. Glanville Williams, pp. 291 ff., 301-2.

[329] Compare Dr. Ganville Williams, pp. 309-310. See also Fletcher, pp. 174-6.

[330] Dr. Glanville Williams, p. 292.

[331] See the address of Pope Pius XII on Religious and Moral Aspects of Pain Prevention in Medical Practice, cited in the last chapter. Compare McFadden, *Medical Ethics,* pp. 140-

158; the Cahiers Laennec studies of Pain, translated and published in *New Problems in Medical Ethics,* III, ed. by Dom Peter Flood, pp. 185-258; F. Petit, *Le mal dans le monde,* in *Initiation théologique,* Eds. du Cerf, Paris, 1957, t. II, pp. 224-246, and *Le problème du mal,* Coll. Je sais, Je crois, Arthaud, Paris, 1958; F. J. J. Buytendijk, *De la douleur,* French transl., Presses Univ. de France, 1951, esp. pp. 144-9; Max Scheler, *Le sens de la souffrance,* pp. 1-71; C. S. Lewis, *The Problem of Pain,* Bles, London, 1940; and many of the leters from Christians awaiting death in Nazi concentration camps, published in *Dying We Live,* ed. by Trevor Huddleston, Harvill, London, 1956.

332 This was the judgment of St. Paul on the contemporary Romans: see *Romans* 1:31.

333 Allen & Unwin, London, 1957.

334 The quotation is from the introduction, written by Russell, to the book called *The New Generation* (1930); the passage is on pp. 121-2 of *Why I am not a Christian.*

335 This is scarcely an adequate defence. Russell evades the point that the horrifying state of affairs described is logically connected with the sexual ethics which he has constantly advocated and of which many of the papers reprinted in this book show him to be an unrepentant advocate.

336 On 21 October, he wrote again: ". . . My own ethics are unsatisfactory. I cannot meet the arguments against absolute ethical values, and yet I cannot believe that a dislike of wanton cruelty is merely a matter of taste, like a dislike of oysters."

337 Allen & Unwin, London.

338 Pp. 27-8. Much of the agnostic's sexual ethics rests on the implied assumption: what we can (thanks to science) do, we may do. (This is a curious reversal of Kant's dictum: I ought implies I can). This assumption has lost all plausability since science has made possible the extermination of civilization by nuclear bombs. Russell should reconsider *Marriage and Morals,* applying to contraceptives the reasoning he now applies to H-bombs.

339 *The Scientific Outlook,* pp. 12, 190, 261, 268, 274-5; compare *Common Sense and Nuclear Warfare,* p. 20.

340 See *The Scientific Outlook,* p. 241: "Christian ethics is in certain fundamental respects opposed to the scientific ethic

. . . Christianity emphasizes the importance of the individual soul and is not prepared to sanction the sacrifice of an innocent man for the sake of some ulterior good to the majority." Compare p. 260: "It may be thought that religion and sentiment will always succeed in opposing an immovable veto to such a system. I wish I could think so." (Cf. p. 229.) In *Human Society in Ethics and Politics,* Allen & Unwin, London, 1954, he wrote (p. 9): "What the world needs is Christian love or compassion." These are extraordinary statements from one who has attacked religion all his life and has certainly been one of the great de-Christianizing influences in our time. In 1957, introducing *Why I am not a Christian,* he vigorously denied "the rumour that (he had) become less opposed to religious orthodoxy than (he) formerly was", and he went on: "I think all the great religions of the world—Buddhism; Hinduism, Christianity, Islam and Communism—*(sic)*—both untrue and harmful."

Index of Subjects

223

Index of Persons

225